THE HISTORY OF NATIONS

China

Other books in the History of Nations series:

England

Germany

THE HISTORY OF NATIONS

China

C.J. Shane, *Book Editor*

Daniel Leone, *President*
Bonnie Szumski, *Publisher*
Scott Barbour, *Managing Editor*

**GREENHAVEN
PRESS®**

THOMSON

GALE

San Diego • Detroit • New York • San Francisco • Cleveland
New Haven, Conn. • Waterville, Maine • London • Munich

Library of Congress, 15

LIBRARY OF CONGRESS CATALOGING-IN-PUBLICATION DATA

China / C.J. Shane, book editor.
   p. cm. — (History of nations)
Includes bibliographical references and index.
   ISBN 0-7377-1193-0 (pbk. : alk. paper) — ISBN 0-7377-1194-9 (lib. : alk. paper)
    1. China—History. 2. China—Foreign relations. I. Shane, C.J. II. History of nations (Greenhaven Press).
DS735. C51138 2003
951—dc21   2002029939

Contents

try. In addition to being a marvel of construction, the Great Wall has been important in the economic, political, and military affairs of the country.

tion in the last days of the Qing empire by attacking foreigners in China. Their violent tactics gave the foreign governments an excuse to send troops into Chinese territory to repress the rebellion.

Chapter 2: Revolution and War: China in the Early Twentieth Century

Chapter 3: China Under Communism

Chapter 4: China in the Twenty-First Century

FOREWORD

I n 1841, the journalist Charles MacKay remarked, "In reading the history of nations, we find that, like individuals, they have their whims and peculiarities, their seasons of excitement and recklessness." At the time of MacKay's observation, many of the nations explored in the Greenhaven Press History of Nations series did not yet exist in their current form. Nonetheless, whether it is old or young, every nation is similar to an individual, with its own distinct characteristics and unique story.

The History of Nations series is dedicated to exploring these stories. Each anthology traces the development of one of the world's nations from its earliest days, when it was perhaps no more than a promise on a piece of paper or an idea in the mind of some revolutionary, through to its status in the world today. Topics discussed include the pivotal political events and power struggles that shaped the country as well as important social and cultural movements. Often, certain dramatic themes and events recur, such as the rise and fall of empires, the flowering and decay of cultures, or the heroism and treachery of leaders. As well, in the history of most countries war, oppression, revolution, and deep social change feature prominently. Nonetheless, the details of such events vary greatly, as does their impact on the nation concerned. For example, England's "Glorious Revolution" of 1688 was a peaceful transfer of power that set the stage for the emergence of democratic institutions in that nation. On the other hand, in China, the overthrow of dynastic rule in 1912 led to years of chaos, civil war, and the eventual emergence of a Communist regime that used violence as a tool to root out opposition and quell popular protest. Readers of the Greenhaven Press History of Nations series will learn about the common challenges nations face and the different paths they take in response to such crises. However a nation's story may have developed, the series strives to present a clear and unbiased view of the country at hand.

The structure of each volume in the series is designed to help students deepen their understanding of the events, movements, and persons that define nations. First, a thematic introduction provides critical background material and helps orient the reader. The chapters themselves are designed to provide an accessible and engaging approach to the study of the history of that nation involved and are arranged either thematically or chronologically, as appropriate. The selections include both primary documents, which convey something of the flavor of the time and place concerned, and secondary material, which includes the wisdom of hindsight and scholarship. Finally, each book closes with a detailed chronology, a comprehensive bibliography of suggestions for further research, and a thorough index.

The countries explored within the series are as old as China and as young as Canada, as distinct in character as Spain and India, as large as Russia, and as compact as Japan. Some are based on ethnic nationalism, the belief in an ethnic group as a distinct people sharing a common destiny, whereas others emphasize civic nationalism, in which what defines citizenship is not ethnicity but commitment to a shared constitution and its values. As human societies become increasingly globalized, knowledge of other nations and of the diversity of their cultures, characteristics, and histories becomes ever more important. This series responds to the challenge by furnishing students with a solid and engaging introduction to the history of the world's nations.

Introduction

More than any other person, Confucius influenced the course of Chinese history. He established a pragmatic moral system and code of behavior designed to create better government and a more harmonious society. Over time, his teachings were modified and expanded by his followers, and they became what historian Jonathan Spence calls "the crystallization of an inherent Chinese wisdom." For over two millennia, Confucian wisdom has been at the foundation of Chinese social and political life. In order to understand Chinese history, it is essential to examine Confucianism and its influence on the nation's leaders and culture through the years.

Confucius, His Teachings, and Chinese Society

Confucius was born Kong Qiu in 551 B.C. in the state of Lu, now the modern province of Shandong. Kong Qiu came to be known as Kong Fuzi, or Master-Teacher Kong. This last name, *Kong Fuzi*, became known as *Confucius* in the West.

Confucius was an intellectual and a teacher who taught two concepts: *li* and *ren*. *Li* was the quality of propriety or proper behavior. *Ren* referred to proper thought or an inward state of benevolence and humanity. These qualities were cultivated by self-improvement through education. Leaders of society, especially rulers, were called on to develop these inward qualities of right thought and behavior. Leadership was based on moral prestige, not law. If the ruler governed with benevolence and humanity, a harmonious society would result. If not, the ruler could lose the right to rule. Scholar-advisers counseled the ruler and helped him to govern in a manner consistent with Confucian values.

The emphasis on proper behavior and thought in Confucian thinking evolved into the concept of five relationships of correct social order: emperor and official, father and son, husband and wife, elder brother and younger brother, and friend and friend. All of these relationships—except the last—were hierarchical. Obedience to those higher in the hierarchy was expected.

These relationships depended on filial submission, loyalty, and reciprocity. Filial piety toward one's parents was the most important virtue. The emperor was considered to be the "father" of the society, and everyone was expected to be obedient to him. Followers of Confucianism believed that if each person observed this social order correctly, then good government and a peaceful society would result.

The Zhou Dynasty and the Hundred Schools of Thought

Of course, Chinese civilization did not begin with Confucius. However, even prior to Confucius, society was organized hierarchically. Under the Xia (2205?–1766? B.C.) and the Shang (1766?–1122? B.C.) dynasties, ancient China was an agriculture-based society of peasants controlled by aristocratic families who ruled regional territories. The aristocrats were loosely connected to the king by kinship and clan ties. Little is known of the Xia. The Shang are remembered for the use of oracle bones to predict the future, for the first renderings of Chinese script, for militarism against neighboring kingdoms, and for the use of human sacrifice in religious rites. Shang religion taught that the gods gave the king the authority to rule.

The last Shang king was so brutally oppressive that Zhou people in the western region of the kingdom began to plot revolution. The Zhou (1122–256 B.C.) developed the idea of the "Mandate of Heaven" to justify deposing the king and overthrowing the Shang dynasty. The Shang ruler had not ruled benevolently, claimed the Zhou, and therefore he had lost the Mandate of Heaven. The Mandate of Heaven concept, according to historian David C. Wright, held that "Heaven [would] approve and sustain a government only as long as it ruled righteously and did not oppress its people. If and when a government turned into a tyranny, the mandate would be withdrawn and the Chinese people would be justified in rising up and overthrowing it."

Like the Shang, the Zhou dynasty eventually began to lose its authority, and China entered a period of social disorder. Confucius was born during the final days of the Zhou dynasty. Despite the political and social turmoil, it was a time of great intellectual creativity known as the Hundred Schools of Thought (ca. 600–300 B.C.). Confucius was only one of many thinkers who promoted new ideas during this time.

Taoism, another of the "Hundred Schools," rejected much of Confucianism's moral order as excessively restrictive. The Taoists looked to the patterns of nature as the answer to problems and believed that a deeper, more intuitive type of knowledge was available to those who opened their hearts. This belief contrasted with the Confucian emphasis on education, intellect, and moral behavior. Taoism became the inspiration for much of China's great arts, painting, poetry, music, and calligraphy, whereas Confucianism inspired the long-standing political and social structures of Chinese society.

Legalism, another important political philosophy of the time, emphasized the rule of law over the Confucian idea of a benevolent sage-king. The rule of law was not democratic, though. It was based entirely on the wishes of the emperor. Cultivation of the individual and creation of a moral social order was of no interest to the Legalists. The strength of the ruler was the ultimate value. Those who did not follow the emperor's law would be severely punished under a Legalist system.

The Legalist system suited Shihuangdi (259–209 B.C.), who is remembered as the man who unified China for the first time. He established the Qin dynasty (221–206 B.C.) and adopted Legal-

Confucius established a moral system and code of behavior that has been at the foundation of Chinese social and political life for over two thousand years.

ism as his state ideology. Emperor Shihuangdi was suspicious of both scholars and merchants, whom he considered parasites. He burned Confucian texts and executed many Confucian scholars during his campaign to consolidate his rule. Shihuangdi wanted to establish a dynasty that would last ten thousand years, but his brutal dynasty was overthrown only a few years after his death.

The Han Adopt Confucianism as the State Ideology

When rebels overthrew the harsh and short-lived Qin dynasty, Liu Bang (247–195 B.C.) emerged as the founder of a new dynasty, the Han (202 B.C.–A.D. 220). The Han dynasty is considered to be China's formative dynasty. Many of the basic social and political structures that would endure for two thousand years were introduced into civic life by the Han. The dynasty was so important to the creation of Chinese civilization that Chinese people today call themselves "Han" or "people of the Han."

Liu Bang was a brilliant military leader, but as an uneducated commoner, he knew that he would need assistance governing his empire. He turned to educated men for counsel, thus incorporating into governance the Confucian idea of the scholar-adviser. In this way, the ancient practice of aristocratic rule over common folk was continued by the Han, but now this tradition, according to historian John K. Fairbank, was "preserved and transmitted through Confucianism. The former aristocrat became the scholar official, and Confucianism his ideology." The role of the Confucian scholar-adviser in this system was to assist the ruler to rule well and retain the Mandate of Heaven. A later Han emperor would establish an examination to select the best among the scholar-advisers. This selection by merit developed later into the Chinese civil service examination system.

The greatest Han emperor, Wudi (156–87 B.C.), officially adopted Confucianism as the Han state ideology. Wudi's idea of Confucianism was expansive and included whatever the emperor thought was needed to maintain Han rule. Wudi also established a national university to study Confucian thought and to produce scholar-advisers and bureaucratic administrators. The result of this effort, according to Fairbank, was the creation of "a new class of administrators who superintended the great public works—dikes and ditches, walls, palaces and granaries—and who drafted peasant labor and collected the land tax." Fairbank further contends that these administrators combined Confucianism and Legalism to produce a new form of imperialism: "These administrators supplanted the hereditary nobility of feudal times and became the backbone of the imperial regime. They incorporated many of the Legalist methods in a new amalgam, imperial Confucianism."

The Han rulers established the Chinese imperial system that would serve China for more than two thousand years until the Qing dynasty (1644–1912) was overthrown in 1911 and the last emperor abdicated in 1912. The core principles of this system were Confucian. What had been one man's ideas on how to create a harmonious society had become the basis for what political scientist Steven M. Goldstein points out was "the longest lived political system in human history."

The Tang Bureaucracy and the Civil Service Examination

Like earlier dynasties, the Han dynastic rule began to disintegrate after four centuries. China entered into a long period of political upheaval known as the Period of Division (A.D. 220–589). The Sui dynasty (589–618) reunified China using militarism and harsh rule. However, the Sui dynasty was quickly overthrown and was followed by China's second great dynasty, the powerful and wealthy Tang (618–907).

Principles of imperial government established by the Han (and based on Confucianism) were expanded and refined by the Tang. Public administration was very adept under Tang emperors. Again, it was the Confucian scholars who acted as advisers to the emperor and as administrators in the imperial government. The bureaucracy was divided into six ministries: civil appointments, revenue (tax collection), rites, war, punishments, and public works. Administering public works involved drafting peasant labor for the construction of palaces and of dikes and canals for flood control and irrigation. Regional territories were organized, and officials were assigned fixed duties within each territory. An inspection system was developed whereby independent officials were sent to check up on provincial bureaucrats. The bureaucracy included more than thirty thousand civil servants, a relatively small size considering the huge population and vast expanses of China.

The imperial bureaucracy had very little direct contact with the villagers in China's countryside. The rural peasants were more directly governed by a local gentry class that both possessed land and held civil service positions. Lower-level civil service positions were sometimes purchased or awarded to the local gentry rather than earned by passing the civil service examination. The gentry class was the intermediary between the imperial bureaucrats and the common people. "Heaven is high and the emperor is far away" was a common saying among Chinese peasants. This administrative structure was remarkably flexible and provided balance between central and local control.

The civil service system that had been established by the Han emperor was expanded and developed during Tang rule. Some scholars believe that the competitive civil service examination and the bureaucracy were among China's greatest contributions to civilization. Any man could take the exam, although women were not permitted to participate. That the examination was open to all men meant that it became a route to upward social mobility for poor families. Some poor men did enter the bureaucracy by performing well on the examination, but the vast majority of those who earned degrees came from the aristocratic class. Only rich aristocrats had the leisure time needed to study enough to pass the test. The course of study for the examination was based on the so-called Four Books and Five Classics. These Confucian texts represented state ideology and were made up of sayings of Confucius and commentaries on his teachings.

This system of administration and recruitment of officials was maintained for many centuries until the final years of imperial rule. Although the bureaucracy made possible the smooth administration of a vast empire, the Confucian scholar-officials were sometimes susceptible to corruption, and nepotism crept into the bureaucracy.

The Last Dynasty

The last imperial dynasty, the Qing (1644–1912), was established by Manchu conquerors from the north. Although the Manchus were outsiders, they left most Confucian political and social institutions virtually unchanged. The Manchus were said to have become "more Chinese than the Chinese." Although the Qing emperors were not descendants of Han Chinese rulers, they legitimized themselves by promoting Confucian values. Saying that they were virtuous rulers and worthy of their subjects' loyalty, the Qing claimed the Mandate of Heaven.

The Qing dynasty, at its height during the eighteenth century, was geographically huge, culturally sophisticated, and very powerful. Its social and political structure was fundamentally Confucian, just as all the dynasties reaching back to the Han had been. According to sociologist Martin K. Whyte,

> Chinese society in late imperial times was shaped by a set of Confucian assumptions and values about the ideal society.... The cement that held society together was supposed to be moral consensus, and the building blocks that were held together by this cement were human bonds and mutual obligations arranged in a vast hierarchy—from emperor and ministers down through local officials and local gentry, and finally to the immediate family—the bonds between father and son, husband and wife, brother and brother, and so on. It was assumed that a uniform "correct" set of values and rules of behavior could be specified for all of the links in this complex human chain of relationships; in the ideal society, systematic instruction in these proper rules, and group pressure to comply with them, would produce social harmony and prosperity.

The fabric of Chinese society was solidly Confucian, but like all dynasties before it, the Qing eventually began to weaken. During the late eighteenth century a population explosion and insufficient food supplies led to a series of rebellions in the empire. Westerners began to appear in China and to make demands for trade concessions. By the middle of the nineteenth century, the emperor was forced to deal with the Taiping Rebellion (1850–1864) and an ensuing civil war that left millions dead. The Qing government also fought and lost a series of wars with Britain, France, and Japan. By the 1890s, China was being called "the sick man of Asia." Now, instead of a new dynasty ready to take over the government, foreigners were waiting to carve up China.

Confucian scholar-advisers to the Qing emperor attempted to respond to these threats to the traditional order by initiating halfhearted reforms in the Self-Strengthening Movement (1861). In 1898 an attempt was made in the Hundred Days Reform to modernize the government, but these reforms also failed. Revolution broke out in 1911, and in 1912 the last Qing emperor abdicated, thus ending imperial rule in China.

The Republican Revolution, New Ideas, and Attacks on Confucianism

The republican revolution was led by Sun Yat-sen (1866–1925). Sun started his political life as a reformer, not a revolutionary. In 1894 he tried to meet with Qing authorities to discuss his reformist ideas, but the authorities refused to see him. Although Sun had a medical degree, he had not earned a degree through the Confucian civil service system. Therefore, his views could not be recommended to the emperor. Sun's reformism was transformed into revolutionary fervor after this blatant rejection by the emperor's advisers. Shortly after the bureaucrats refused to see him, Sun formed a secret revolutionary group called the Revive China Society; he began developing his own political philosophy, which he called the Three Principles of the People: nationalism, socialism, and democracy. For nearly twenty years, Sun worked tirelessly to build support for a revolution in China.

The revolution finally broke out in 1911 in the city of Wuhan. When the last emperor abdicated and the Qing dynasty passed into history, a weak and disorganized republican government emerged, led briefly by Sun and later by Yuan Shihkai (1859–1916). Yuan was a strong leader with military backing, but after his death in 1916, no equally strong leader emerged to hold the country together. China degenerated into the "warlord period" (1916–1927), during which regional military leaders vied for control of the nation.

Despite the tremendous political changes generated by the 1911 revolution, the fundamental underlying values of Chinese society, and the life of the average Chinese person, changed very little during this period. Family traditions persisted, and peasants continued to work the land as they had done for centuries. British historian J.A.G. Roberts says, "The 1911 revolution had dismantled the political framework of the Confucian state, but the Confucian tradition remained dominant in the family." The emperor was gone, but Confucian values remained intact in Chinese homes and villages.

This was not the case among China's urban intellectuals. Out of the political chaos of the early republican era there developed a renaissance in thought that is often compared to the Hundred Schools of Thought period (600–300 B.C.) that produced Confucianism. The intellectuals leading this revolution had been educated in the West and were the first to launch a spirited attack on Confucianism. They were leaders of the intellectual New Cultural Movement and an associated nationalistic political movement called the May Fourth Movement.

Intellectuals Cai Yuanpei and Hu Shi pointed to Confucianism as a significant cause of China's problems. Hu Shi wanted to replace Confucianism with "Mr. Science and Mr. Democracy." Wu Yu attacked filial piety, which he saw as the basis of loyalty to a despotic emperor. Chen Duxiu attacked Confucianism frequently in the pages of his magazine, *New Youth*. Chen associated Confucianism with a feudal society that was holding back China's economic, social, and political development. Chen called for fundamental social changes, including doing away with class hierarchies and improving the status of women. Chen eventually turned to Marxist-Leninism and became a founding member of the Chinese Communist Party (CCP).

Communism and Confucianism

One of the first to join the new CCP was a young man named Mao Zedong (1893–1976). Mao had been born into a rural farming family in Hunan Province, moved to Beijing, and associated himself with leaders of the New Cultural Movement and May Fourth Movement. Mao and the CCP began to formulate a vision of a new China that rejected Confucianism, which the Communists identified as feudal.

Before the Communists could enact a new social agenda, they had to defeat both the Japanese invaders and the Nationalist Party troops led by Chiang Kai-shek (1887–1975). Chiang had aligned himself with the traditional Confucian social order. He launched the New Life Movement in 1934, which promoted Confucian virtues, and he established a national holiday to honor Confucius's birthday. The attempt to preserve the old order failed when Chiang and the Nationalists were defeated by the Communists in a civil war (1947–1949). The victorious Chinese Communist Party established the People's Republic of China in 1949, and Chiang Kai-shek fled to the island of Taiwan.

Mao Zedong and his comrades set about creating a new society based on Marxist-Leninist, not Confucian, ideals. Among the most important aspects of Mao's social program were land reform and destruction of the landed gentry class. Mao believed that the old hierarchical, feudal, and patriarchal society had to be transformed. Women were to be equal partners in building the new society. New laws affecting marriage, children, labor, and education dramatically improved the status of women and of the common peasant. Sweeping reforms on every level were instituted, and the entire society was mobilized for change. Not all reforms worked. The Great Leap Forward (1957–1962), Mao's program to improve agricultural and industrial output, was a disaster. Famine resulted, and millions of peasants died of starvation.

By the mid-1960s Mao's failed policies had made him unpopular, and he was rapidly losing political influence. In response, he encouraged the unleashing of the Cultural Revolution (1966–1976), a mass movement dedicated to returning China to revolutionary principles. Gangs of youths called the Red Guard carried out Mao's revolutionary initiatives. "To rebel is justified" was the Red Guard slogan. Confucianism came under even more virulent attack during the Cultural Revolution. Everything old and everything that had been valued under a traditional Confucian society were rejected, including scholarship. Intellectuals and scholars were particularly brutalized. Many schools closed. Teachers were removed from their positions and banished to rural areas to work as farm laborers. Confucian shrines were attacked and destroyed by the Red Guard. Anyone perceived to be an enemy of Mao was linked to Confucianism and attacked. A political rival of Mao's named Lin Biao (1907–1971) was attacked during the Anti-Confucius and Anti–Lin Biao Campaign.

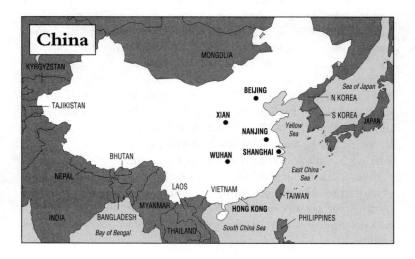

Despite the overt rejection of Confucianism, Communist society under Mao developed some striking parallels to the old dynastic society. The imperial bureaucracy was replaced by a large Communist bureaucracy. Political connections in Communist China became just as important as the right social relations had been in earlier times. In many ways, Mao filled the role of emperor. During the Cultural Revolution, he became a cult figure; his picture was placed in every home, and every day the common people wished him a "thousand years." Mao's *Quotations* (commonly called the Little Red Book) were memorized and quoted with the same fervor that Confucius's writings had once been studied and quoted.

Even the Confucian idea of self-cultivation through education appeared in the Communist legal system as the concept of "reform through education." Legal scholar Victor Li writes that Communist China uses two models of law. The "external model" is based on a formal written legal code. According to Li, in the

> internal model proper modes of behavior are taught not through written laws, but rather through a lengthy and continuing educational process whereby a person first learns and then internalizes the socially accepted values and norms.... This model seems to include many traditional Chinese ideas and practices. Especially striking is its similarity to the concept of *li*. Both rely heavily upon persuasion and education rather than force. Indeed, if one substitutes the term "socialist morality" for "Confucian morality" and the term "comrade" for "*chun-tzu*" (gentleman), one can use some of the Chinese classics to describe this model of law.

Mao's death in 1976 brought an end to the Cultural Revolution and the attacks on Confucianism. Many Chinese citizens who had been attacked and purged during the ten years before Mao's death were now set to be rehabilitated.

The New Confucianism and Deng's Revolution

Confucius was among those who were rehabilitated after the Cultural Revolution. As early as 1979, government funds were appropriated to restore Confucian shrines that had been destroyed by the Red Guard. Qufu in Shandong Province is the ancestral home of Confucius. During the Cultural Revolution the town was attacked, Confucian shrines and temples were burned, and statues were defaced by the Red Guard. The government restored these shrines, and today Qufu is a popular tourist attraction. Many Chinese visit Qufu every year on Confucius's birthday, September 28, to honor him.

Academics in China today have taken up the study of Confucian texts, and conferences are organized to analyze his teachings. Several Chinese universities also offer degree programs in Confucian studies. In 2002 more than 2 million Chinese schoolchildren studied the Confucian classics. This growing interest in traditional Confucian values is being called the New Confucianism.

Sweeping economic reforms initiated by Deng Xiaoping (1904–1997) during the 1980s and 1990s created yet another revolution in Chinese society. Declaring "to get rich is glorious," Deng opened China to the West and to Western technology and markets, relaxed central bureaucratic controls on the economy, and established "special economic zones." This economic revolution has sometimes been termed the *second liberation* (the first being the establishment of the People's Republic of China). Some believe it may ultimately prove to be more significant than the Communist revolution. As a result of Deng's reforms, the Chinese economy grew rapidly, and the standard of living for the average Chinese citizen dramatically improved in only a few short years. Political reform has not accompanied economic reform at the same pace, however, and tensions caused by the disparity plague contemporary Chinese society.

The spectacular economic growth that has occurred during the last generation has been attributed in part to the Confucian code of behavior and values. As scholar William Theodore de Bary writes, the "Confucian work ethic, social discipline, and zeal for learning" have come to be recognized as contributing significantly to China's recent economic successes. Heritage Foundation scholar Julian Weiss writes, "Since the mid-1980s [Confucianism] has been generally praised for its contribution to Asia's 'miracle' of economic growth. The teachings are seen as at odds with individualism, yet paradoxically they rely on individual will and moral character. A moral government, filial piety, and benevolence are also core values."

The appeal of Confucianism stems from more than its association with economic success. Stephen Yates, a scholar at the Heritage Foundation, says that there is a "moral void" in China today. "The government can't fill this void," says Yates, "nor can making money." In fact, the creation of wealth in China is yet one more of "the forces of assimilation and modernization that threaten the Chinese sense of culture and chang-tong (continuity)," according to Weiss. Confucianism resists these forces and adheres to the traditional Chinese wisdom. In addition, for many Chinese, Confucian values contrast favorably with what is seen as the excessive individualism and decadence of the West.

It is not possible to say exactly where Confucianism will lead Chinese society in the future. We can say for certain, though, that Confucian values and principles have been integral to the fabric of Chinese society and essential Chinese wisdom for more than two millennia. There is every reason to believe that the teachings of Confucius will continue to influence Chinese civilization.

*   *   *   *   *

A Note on Chinese Pinyin Language

Chinese written language is readable to Chinese people everywhere regardless of the dialect spoken. However, Chinese language makes little sense to Westerners unless they are trained to read the characters. Systems of transliterating these characters—that is, changing them into a different alphabet—have been developed to make it possible for Westerners to read Chinese.

There are two systems of transliteration. The Wade-Giles system was used for many years, and this system is still found in many older books. The pinyin system was officially adopted by the Chinese government during the 1950s and is used everywhere today in China. When pinyin was established, names such as *Peking* under the Wade-Giles system became *Beijing. Mao Tse-tung* became *Mao Zedong*.

For Westerners, there are two important pronunciation keys: The pinyin *q* is pronounced "ch," and *x* is pronounced as "sh." Therefore, *Qing* is pronounced "Ching," and *Xia* is pronounced "Shia."

This book generally uses the pinyin system. However, if an article was written using the Wade-Giles system, that system is retained, and pinyin names are included in parentheses. Exceptions to this are names that are very well known under the Wade-Giles system, such as *Chiang Kai-shek* and *Sun Yat-sen*.

Regarding Chinese names: The surname (family name) is given first and the personal name follows. For example, *Mao* is Mao Zedong's surname.

THE HISTORY OF NATIONS
Chapter 1

Dynastic Rule

The Shang and Zhou Dynasties

By Ray Huang

The first dynasty recorded in China's historical writings was the Xia (2205 B.C.?–1763 B.C.?). There is little archaeological evidence for this culture, although there are many stories and legends about it. Following the Xia were the Shang (1766 B.C.–1122 B.C.) and Zhou (1122 B.C.–256 B.C.) dynasties. The Shang people are remembered for their use of oracle bones to divine the future. The Chinese writing system began to develop during the Shang period.

During the Zhou dynasty, a social and economic system called fengjian *was established that had some similarities to European feudalism. Historian Ray Huang, in this selection from his* China: A Macro History, *describes* fengjian. *The system was characterized by hereditary lords tied together by kinship relations who ruled over agrarian lands worked by peasants. Toward the end of the Zhou rule, the power of the central government declined and turmoil followed. There was so much warfare among the agrarian states that the later Zhou era is known as the Warring States period.*

Huang is the author of 1587: A Year of No Significance, *which was nominated for an American Book Award. He served ten years in the Chinese National Army and taught at the State University of New York.*

The designation of the Shang as a "dynasty" is not a misnomer, as the genealogy of the ruling house exists and the succession of the kings is known to have taken place by and large from brother to brother and, on fewer occasions, from father to son, always within the extended family. But otherwise the Shang appear to be a people who, with their mastery of bronze technology, assumed overlordship over many other peoples on the strength of their military superiority and religious cohesion. The extant bronze objects of the Shang, with few exceptions, are weapons and sacrificial vessels. They were produced in centralized manufacturing plants under state sponsorship.

Many Shang characteristics would have marked it as being closer to other cultures on a similar standing rather than as being distinctly Chinese. For example, although it was a patriarchal society, the Shang allowed its aristocratic women a degree of freedom and equality with men not attained by the daughters of China many centuries and even millenniums later. The Shang people were cheerful and robust, and they consumed large quantities of alcoholic beverages. They practiced human sacrifice and felt no qualms about it, as they routinely and unsentimentally recorded such deeds on the oracle bones. They were able to dispatch an army of 3,000 men on a marching expedition of 100 days. And this army could be augmented by forces contributed by Shang vassals. Sometimes they waged war for profit. The burial sites of Shang kings featured a series of pits one inside another, huge on top and progressively smaller as they were executed downward. Buried along with the remains of the kings were chariots and horses and human beings, some of them decapitated and arranged in formations. The pounded earth steps leading downward suggest elaborate rituals at the funeral services.

We believe that the Shang people, while versed in agriculture, maintained a strong pastoral tradition. In their 500-odd years of history, they moved their capital more than half a dozen times, and hunting is often mentioned on the oracle bones. Yet some scholars believe that they moved their capital to a different site because the mineral resources on the nearby mountains had been exhausted for manufacturing weapons and religious objects. It is difficult to say which theory holds more truth. Near modern Anyang, where the last Shang capital was located, archaeologists have discovered bones of wild animals in great variety. Food production, on the other hand, seems to have been relegated to slave labor; in one pit alone stone sickles have been found by the thousands.

Engravings on the oracle bones indicate that the Shang kings had a special concern for the weather. Calendar making was an essential function of the royal court, and in fact, all the Shang kings were named after the index divisions that formed a calendar cycle. In these respects the Shang dynasty begins to connect with agrarian China. Yet the strongest link between the Shang and the subsequent Chinese cultural tradition is the writing system found on the oracle bones.

Originally, these pieces were scribed for divination, but most of those extant today were reproduced by the Shang archivists as a permanent record. Thus large numbers of them have been unearthed, yielding a great deal of information about a nucleus state on the threshold of becoming a significant civilization. Specialists have counted some 3,000 different characters on the bone surfaces, and of these close to 1,000 have been decoded. . . .

Zhou Dynasty

During the reign of the last Shang king, the Zhou, either by overbearing power or by impartial arbitration, had won the allegiance of a number of states that were supposedly subordinate to the Shang. The extension of Zhou influence into the Han River region leading to the Yangtze Valley in particular threatened the southern flank of the Shang on the Eastern Plain. Clashes between the Shang and Zhou ensued. The Zhou chief of state, Xibai, was for a time imprisoned by the Shang but later was ransomed off.

It was one of Xibai's sons who finally organized an eastward expedition in collaboration with a large number of rebelling Shang vassals to terminate the Shang overlordship and replace it with the Zhou dynasty. This took place either in 1027 B.C. or 1122 B.C., depending on which school of chronology one chooses to follow. . . .

The heroic figure who became the progenitor of a royal house that was to last for 800 years, however, never claimed to be the dynastic founder. That honor was given to his father, Xibai, who was posthumously proclaimed King Wen, or the "cultured king," in commemoration of his humility and statesmanship. His son, the leader of the military expedition, whose personal name is Fa, is in turn known to history by his posthumous title, King Wu, or the "martial king." The moral lessons that sons should never make claims so grand as to overshadow their fathers and that virtue and the doctrine of harmony must triumph over military exploits became a tradition ever after, although more often the doctrine was given lip service rather than substantiated by deeds.

We have reason to believe that the Zhou was inferior to the Shang in bronze technology. With the fall of the overlordship on the Eastern Plain the brilliancy in metal design and craftsmanship seems to have been permanently lost. But with the rise of the new rulers from the loess land, China developed a large body of classical literature, some portions of which still make interesting reading nowadays. Primogeniture now replaced the Shang practice of fraternal succession. Religious differences between the two cultures were sharp. The animism of the Shang disappeared with the emergence of the Zhou, and even though ancestor worship continued, the earlier beliefs and expectations that made individual ancestors responsible for their descendants' successes and failures across a wide range of activities, from winning a war to nursing a troublesome tooth, were replaced by the honoring of lineage origin and the guaranteeing of its perpetuation as an obligation of posterity. Some writers have suggested racial differences between the Shang and the Zhou. But if an ethnic difference existed, it could not have been profound, as the written language does not show a notable break with the dynastic change. More convincing is the explanation that the culture developed in the loess land had a greater agrarian influence. The loess terrace, as some scholars reason, may have been the birthplace of China's agriculture. The long list of plants cited in a collection of folk songs dating from the early Zhou seems to give credence to the claim.

In any case, the Zhou founders proved to be the greatest system-builders of China's formative age. The Duke of Zhou, son of King Wen and younger brother of King Wu, is credited with being the chief architect of the state institutions under the new dynasty. To this day historians have reached no consensus regarding his overall design. But there is little doubt that the duke's organization was schematic. The preconceived mathematical concepts usually came with geometric patterns. Sweeping yet simple, the audacious designs were superimposed on a vast country before a single land survey was made or a census taken to test their feasibility. . . .

The *Fengjian* System

The Zhou system, called *fengjian* in Chinese, is always rendered "feudal" in English. The similarity between European "feudalism" and *fengjian* exists only in some aspects, and rather more in spirit than in substance. Generally speaking, against an agrarian background they both entrusted local government to the hands of hereditary lords. The territorial lords under the Zhou king were commissioned from the kin of the royal house, descendants of the vanquished Shang, and chiefs of other tribal states already in existence. They were divided into five ranks according to the size of their domains, which were in theory standardized. Their functions and duties to the king varied by the distance of their fiefs from the royal capital. They were supposed to reside within nine belts of land, which formed huge square frameworks concentric with the capital city. In practice, no such territorial division could be drawn on the map. Nor had Xi'an, the capital, actually been situated at the center up to this time.

Aside from such bold but unrealistic concepts, however, many innovations of the Duke of Zhou can be verified, sometimes even in detail. The paradox is not difficult to explain: The overarching principles of state-building are expected to bring forth an ideal perfection in conforming with the Natural Law. While deviations are as a rule accepted, the lower echelon nonetheless must at first strive to achieve the projected symmetry and balance to the best of its ability. For that pressure is constantly exerted from the top. In the long run, however, it is fitting that China is becoming a country of political thinkers under the influence of a bureaucratic management that habitually gives a priori recognition to form rather than to substance. What started as a technical necessity has become Natural Law itself after prolonged usage.

Another example of the Duke of Zhou's innovations was the alignment of his type of feudalism with kinship relationships. In every fief the family temple of the lord functioned as a kind of territorial shrine. The patron ancestor held the entire population together to form a pseudo-kinship. (A legacy from this arrangement is that today dozens of Chinese surnames trace their origin to those tribal states.) Within each unit, not only was the position of the lord hereditary, but also, his councillors and ministers always came from the designated noble lineages, who took possession of estates within the fief mandated at the founding of the dynasty. Those nobles assumed military leadership as well. In the early phase of the Zhou, the warrior-administrator caste was separated from the general population.

Under the Zhou, the cultivated fields were supposed to be arranged according to a "well-field system." A "well" consisted of about forty acres of land in a perfect square. By a division of three on each side, the entire field was gridded into nine equal parts of about four and a half acres each. Eight peasant families occupied the peripheral subdivisions and jointly cultivated the center square, which was the lord's demesne. The arrangement, not necessarily carried out precisely as described, seems to have been in effect in wide regions. Evidently, in those days the peasant populace regarded their unpaid labor on the lord's demesne to be a public obligation. A lingering effect of this practice in the current Chinese language, somewhat curiously, is that the same character is used to mean both "the public" and "lordship."

Zhou Decline and the Warring States

To say that the Zhou introduced feudalism to China may be misleading. Rather, with *fengjian* the new dynasty installed a mode of government that was congenial to the spread of agriculture at the time. The alignment with kinship relationships contributed to its stability. The ideology of peaceful coexistence, which many centuries later was to be labeled "Confucian," owed a great deal to King Wen and the Duke of Zhou, as Confucius himself admitted. The devotion to ritual and the obsession with form rather than substance, as previously mentioned, were to be passed on to agrarian China for millenniums to come. Indeed, the Zhou did not take hold of China for 800 formative years without leaving a permanent imprint. Its enduring influence is such that for historians it is often difficult to determine whether a characteristic under discussion is that of the Zhou or that of the Chinese.

But at the top of a league of agrarian states in a sprawling country, the house of Zhou exercised effective overlordship for no more than 250 years. During the early centuries new fields were opened; " barbarian" tribes that continued fishing and hunting as their major methods of gathering food were converted and brought within the pale of civilization. From its vassals the Zhou collected tribute, and the arbitration of disputes by the court was effective. But by the early eighth century B.C., if not earlier, these positive attributes were gradually slipping away. In 771 B.C. the Zhou capital at modern Xi'an was ransacked by an invading tribe, which also killed the king. When the crown prince resettled in the east, the dynasty, now known as the Eastern Zhou, was set for a long period of decline. In the meantime, the royal domain fell into the hands of the Qin, nominally still a Zhou vassal.

Traditionally, this era of diminishing royal power is presented in history in two distinctive but not chronologically connected segments. They are the "Spring and Autumn Period" (722 B.C.–481 B.C.) and the "Period of the Warring States" (403 B.C.–221 B.C.), to conform to the time span of two classical history works. *The Spring and Autumn Annals* is a state chronicle; the *Strategy of the Warring States* is a collection of anecdotes at the court level. Both are brilliantly composed.

Confucianism and Other Philosophies of the Zhou Dynasty

By the Library of Congress

Warfare and social disruption characterized much of the Zhou dynasty. At the same time, the intellectual ferment of the period gave rise to many competing philosophies. This "golden age" for Chinese intellectual discourse is known as the time of "The Hundred Schools of Thought."

The most significant school to come out of this period was Confucianism. Based on the ideas of Kong Zi (Confucius), this philosophy was to have the most profound effect on government, society, and moral values in China for more than two millennia. At the same time that Confucianism was developing, competing philosophies emerged. In this article, the Library of Congress describes the growth of Confucianism and other schools of thought, including Legalism, later adopted as a philosophy of governance, and Taoism, which significantly contributed to much of Chinese art and philosophy.

The Spring and Autumn [770–476 B.C.] and Warring States periods [475–221 B.C.], though marked by disunity and civil strife, witnessed an unprecedented era of cultural prosperity—the "golden age" of China. The atmosphere of reform and new ideas was attributed to the struggle for survival among warring regional lords who competed in building strong and loyal armies and in increasing economic production to ensure a broader base for tax collection. To effect these economic, military, and cultural developments, the regional lords needed ever-increasing numbers of skilled, literate officials and teachers,

Library of Congress, "The Hundred Schools of Thought," *China: A Country Study*, 1987.

the recruitment of whom was based on merit. Also during this time, commerce was stimulated through the introduction of coinage and technological improvements. Iron came into general use, making possible not only the forging of weapons of war but also the manufacture of farm implements. Public works on a grand scale—such as flood control, irrigation projects, and canal digging—were executed. Enormous walls were built around cities and along the broad stretches of the northern frontier.

So many different philosophies developed during the late Spring and Autumn and early Warring States periods that the era is often known as that of the Hundred Schools of Thought. From the Hundred Schools of Thought came many of the great classical writings on which Chinese practices were to be based for the next two and one-half millennia. Many of the thinkers were itinerant intellectuals who, besides teaching their disciples, were employed as advisers to one or another of the various state rulers on the methods of government, war, and diplomacy.

Confucius and Mencius

The body of thought that had the most enduring effect on subsequent Chinese life was that of the School of Literati (ru), often called the Confucian school in the West. The written legacy of the School of Literati is embodied in the Confucian Classics, which were to become the basis for the order of traditional society. Confucius (551–479 B.C.), also called Kong Zi, or Master Kong, looked to the early days of Zhou rule for an ideal social and political order. He believed that the only way such a system could be made to work properly was for each person to act according to prescribed relationships. "Let the ruler be a ruler and the subject a subject," he said, but he added that to rule properly a king must be virtuous. To Confucius, the functions of government and social stratification were facts of life to be sustained by ethical values. His ideal was the junzi (ruler's son), which came to mean gentleman in the sense of a cultivated or superior man.

Mencius (372–289 B.C.), or Meng Zi, was a Confucian disciple who made major contributions to the humanism of Confucian thought. Mencius declared that man was by nature good. He expostulated the idea that a ruler could not govern without the people's tacit consent and that the penalty for unpopular, despotic rule was the loss of the "mandate of heaven."

The effect of the combined work of Confucius, the codifier

and interpreter of a system of relationships based on ethical behavior, and Mencius, the synthesizer and developer of applied Confucian thought, was to provide traditional Chinese society with a comprehensive framework on which to order virtually every aspect of life.

There were to be accretions to the corpus of Confucian thought, both immediately and over the millennia, and from within and outside the Confucian school. Interpretations made to suit or influence contemporary society made Confucianism dynamic while preserving a fundamental system of model behavior based on ancient texts.

Legalism

Diametrically opposed to Mencius, for example, was the interpretation of Xun Zi (ca. 300–237 B.C.), another Confucian follower. Xun Zi preached that man is innately selfish and evil and that goodness is attainable only through education and conduct befitting one's status. He also argued that the best government is one based on authoritarian control, not ethical or moral persuasion.

Xun Zi's unsentimental and authoritarian inclinations were developed into the doctrine embodied in the School of Law (fa), or Legalism. The doctrine was formulated by Han Fei Zi (d. 233 B.C.) and Li Si (d. 208 B.C.), who maintained that human nature was incorrigibly selfish and therefore the only way to preserve the social order was to impose discipline from above and to enforce laws strictly. The Legalists exalted the state and sought its prosperity and martial prowess above the welfare of the common people. Legalism became the philosophic basis for the imperial form of government. When the most practical and useful aspects of Confucianism and Legalism were synthesized in the Han period (206 B.C.–A.D. 220), a system of governance came into existence that was to survive largely intact until the late nineteenth century.

Taoism, Yin-Yang, and Five Elements

Taoism (or Daoism in pinyin), the second most important stream of Chinese thought, also developed during the Zhou period. Its formulation is attributed to the legendary sage Lao Zi (Old Master), said to predate Confucius, and Zhuang Zi (369-286 B.C.). The focus of Taoism is the individual in nature rather than the individual in society. It holds that the goal of life for each individual is to find one's own personal adjustment to the rhythm of the natural (and supernatural) world, to follow the Way (dao) of the universe. In many ways the opposite of rigid Confucian moralism, Taoism served many of its adherents as a complement to their ordered daily lives. A scholar on duty as an official would usually follow Confucian teachings but at leisure or in retirement might seek harmony with nature as a Taoist recluse.

Another strain of thought dating to the Warring States Period is the school of yin-yang and the five elements. The theories of this school attempted to explain the universe in terms of basic forces in nature, the complementary agents of yin (dark, cold, female, negative) and yang (light, hot, male, positive) and the five elements (water, fire, wood, metal, and earth). In later periods these theories came to have importance both in philosophy and in popular belief.

Moism

Still another school of thought was based on the doctrine of Mo Zi (470–391 B.C.?), or Mo Di. Mo Zi believed that "all men are equal before God" and that mankind should follow heaven by practicing universal love. Advocating that all action must be utilitarian, Mo Zi condemned the Confucian emphasis on ritual and music. He regarded warfare as wasteful and advocated pacifism. Mo Zi also believed that unity of thought and action were necessary to achieve social goals. He maintained that the people should obey their leaders and that the leaders should follow the will of heaven. Although Moism failed to establish itself as a major school of thought, its views are said to be "strongly echoed" in Legalist thought. In general, the teachings of Mo Zi left an indelible impression on the Chinese mind.

An Assassination Attempt on the Qin Ruler

By Sima Qian (Szuma Chien)

Qin (Chen) dynasty emperor Qin Shihuang (259–209 B.C.) is remembered as the first ruler of a unified China. He standardized weights, measures, and coins, adopted the Chinese script, and established a government administration based on merit, not heredity. Some scholars credit him for initiating construction of the Great Wall of China, although others dispute this claim. His tomb near Xi'an is filled with thousands of life-size terra cotta warriors and is one of the world's great archaeological sites.

Qin Shihuang was not a popular ruler. His brutal conquest of neighboring kingdoms and absolutely ruthless suppression of all opposition made him the target of several assassination attempts. Han-era Grand Historian Sima Qian (Szuma Chien) (145?–90? B.C.) recounts here a failed attempt made on Qin Shihuang's life by the assassin Jing Ke (Ching Ko), who was sent by the ruler of the kingdom of Yen. To gain entrance to the palace, the assassin brought the head of a rival military leader, Fan Yu-chi. Efforts to resist Qin expansion failed. Within five years, the king of Yen had been murdered by Qin Shihuang and Yen was absorbed into the Qin empire.

Sima Qian was a historian during the Han dynasty (202 B.C.– A.D. 220). When he publicly disagreed with Han Wudi (156–87 B.C.), the Han emperor ordered Sima Qian to be castrated. Scholars believe that Han Wudi's intention was to force Sima Qian to commit suicide out of humiliation. Sima Qian chose instead to accept the punishment so that he could live to finish his great historical work, Shi ji.

He [Prince Tan] had been searching for a fine dagger and found one made by Hsu Fu-jen of Chao, which cost a hundred pieces of gold. Now he made his artisans temper this dagger in poison, and upon testing it found that if it drew blood—be it only a drop sufficient to stain a thread—the result was instant death. Then Prince Tan helped Ching Ko [Jing Ke] to prepare for his journey. In Yen there lived a bold youth of thirteen named Chin Wu-yang, a killer from whose angry glance everyone shrank. He was chosen as Ching Ko's assistant. . . .

Upon reaching Chin, Ching Ko bribed the king's favourite, the chamberlain Meng Chia, with money and gifts worth a thousand pieces of gold. And Meng Chia explained his mission to the king.

"The king of Yen trembles before your might and dares not oppose your troops," he said. "He begs to become your subject like the other princes and send tribute like your provinces, in order to continue his ancestral sacrifices. He was afraid to come in person to announce this, but he has cut off Fan Yu-chi's [rival military leader] head to present to you in a sealed casket with the map of Tukang in Yen. The envoy who brought these here is awaiting Your Majesty's orders."

Very pleased at this, the king of Chin prepared a grand reception in Hsienyang Palace to receive the envoy from Yen. Ching Ko entered first with the sealed casket containing Fan Yu-chi's head, followed by Chin Wu-yang with the map case. When they reached the steps to the dais, the ministers were surprised to see Chin Wu-yang change colour and tremble; but Ching Ko stepped forward with a laugh to apologize, saying, "He is a rough country fellow from the barbarous north who is overawed by his first sight of Your Majesty. Please excuse him so that we can carry out our mission."

The king bade Ching Ko hand him the map which Chin Wu-yang was holding, and he unrolled it to reveal the dagger. Ching Ko seized the king's sleeve with his left hand, snatching up the dagger to stab him with his right. Before he could strike, however, the king leapt up in alarm and his sleeve tore off. He tried to draw his long sword but it stuck in the scabbard, and in his panic he could not pull it out. The king fled behind a pillar with Ching Ko in hot pursuit, while the ministers, taken by surprise, were thrown into confusion.

According to the law of Chin, ministers were forbidden to bear arms in the audience hall and the royal guards in the courtyard could not enter without orders from their sovereign; but the king in his panic did not call for them. So while Ching Ko pursued the king, the panic-stricken ministers, having no weapons, tried to ward him off with their bare hands; and the king's physician, Hsia Wu-chu, used his bag of herbs to beat the assassin off. Too terrified to know what to do, the king was running round the pillar when some attendants shouted:

"Put the sword over your shoulder, Your Majesty!"

He did so and, drawing his sword, struck Ching Ko a blow that shattered his left leg. Unable to move, Ching Ko hurled his dagger at the king, but missed him and hit the bronze pillar instead. The king struck again and again, inflicting eight wounds. Then, knowing that all was up with him, Ching Ko squatted against the pillar with a scornful smile.

"I failed through trying to take you alive," he swore. "And because I was determined to force you to agree to our prince's demands!"

At that, attendants ran forward and finished him off. The king brooded in silence for a while, then rewarded those who had been of service and punished others. His physician, Hsia Wu-chu, received two hundred pieces of gold for his loyalty.

China's Great Dynasties: From the Han to the Qing

By Akira Iriye

After Emperor Qin Shi Huang died in 209 B.C., his Qin dynasty fell apart in only a few years. For the next two millennia, China was ruled by a series of great dynasties starting with the Han and ending with the Qing. This last dynasty was overthrown in 1911.

Professor Akira Iriye reviews the contributions of these formidable dynasties to the development of Chinese civilization. Iriye notes the official adoption of Confucianism as a political philosophy and how this philosophy evolved under different dynasties. He reviews the establishment of the civil service examination system, technological advances such as the invention of papermaking and printing, and numerous cultural achievements. Also noteworthy is the tribute system developed by the different dynasties that required regions such as Tibet, Korea, and Vietnam to pay tribute to China.

Iriye is former chair of the history department at the University of Chicago. His book Power and Culture: The Japanese–American War, 1941–1945 *was nominated for a Pulitzer Prize in 1981.*

Han Dynasty (202 B.C.–220 A.D.)

Emerging from the chaos which followed the collapse of the Ch'in [Qin] a new dynasty calling itself Han assumed power in 202 B.C. and proceeded to build a new state. Because Ch'in harshness and brutality had caused their overthrow, the Han carefully avoided imitating the extreme methods of their

Akira Iriye, *The World of Asia*. Arlington Heights, IL: The Forum Press, 1979.

predecessors. To despise Ch'in excesses, however, did not mean abandoning those institutions and practices which had proved so successful in unifying the country and re-establishing order and centralized government. Some aspects of Legalism [which advocated authoritarian government] may have been distasteful to the new regime (the early leaders of which were inclined more toward Taoism), but there was no denying that as far as the daily practice of politics was concerned, Legalism more than any of the other major philosophies seemed more realistic.

On the one hand, then, the organizational structure and administrative practices of the new regime remained rooted in Legalistic thinking. Not long after taking power, however, the Han leadership realized that Legalism could not by itself, unless implemented in the Ch'in manner, be the ideological basis of society. As a result, the government very quickly invited Confucian scholars into official service. After that, Confucianism (not unaffected by the other major schools of thought) gradually rose to such prominence that it was finally declared the state ideology in 124 B.C. With the introduction of a Confucian curriculum into the national university founded in that same year and with the somewhat later (6 A.D.) establishment of a competitive civil service examination system based on Confucian writings, the Confucianization of Chinese culture and politics was well under way....

Before leaving the Han we should mention that the dynasty fulfilled the concept of China as the "Middle Kingdom" (or *Chung-kuo*—"right in the middle"—China as the center of the universe) by pacifying the barbarian tribes on all its frontiers. Imperial forces defeated the Hsiung-nu (Huns) in the north and extended dominion in the south into coastal Annam and Tonkin, present-day Vietnam. Late in the dynasty's history, the Han imperium reached westward to the Caspian Sea and, in so doing, activated trade with Europe via Sinkiang and Central Asia along what became known as the "silk route."...

Sui and Tang Dynasties (581–906 A.D.)

Despite the collapse of the Han dynasty and with it all remnants of central administration in China, the idea of empire survived (particularly in the south) to be resuscitated in the late sixth century by a barbarian, but Sinicized, northern state, the Sui. The effort to reunite the country, however, so exhausted the new dynasty that it was unable to retain the throne for more than a generation. Like the Ch'in before it, though, the Sui prepared the way for the establishment of a much more powerful and long-lived dynasty, the T'ang (618–906 A.D.), which led China to new heights of cultural, economic, military, and administrative achievements.

The T'ang extended the empire's frontiers to their greatest limits yet attained. Campaigns led to the inclusion of Korea, parts of Manchuria, Tonkin, and the areas of present-day Sinkiang and Tibet under China's sway as imperial armies everywhere subdued barbarian neighbors and forced them to acknowledge the Chinese emperor as their overlord. The pattern of diplomatic relations that developed between these peoples and China became an institution known as the tributary system. Originated by the Han, this system allowed foreign peoples to retain their native leaders yet secure Chinese protection in return for periodic tribute in the form of native products (largely symbolic) and homage rendered to the emperor in the imperial capital in recognition of the superiority of the ruler of the Middle Kingdom. . . .

The government sought to deal with the age-old problem of land hunger by reviving the ancient well-field system and distributing public lands among the vastly-increased number of tax-paying peasants as soon as each reached adult status. Government subsidies further assisted China's farmers. The T'ang made no effort, however, to break up the estates of large landowners. Despite providing some relief for small cultivators, the well-field system in the long run could not cope with the continued rise in population and collapsed after the fall of the T'ang.

Several significant innovations were made in the spheres of administration and governmental operations. First, although the T'ang drew upon patterns and institutions established under the Han, they did improve organization by the creation of new offices to handle imperial affairs. Secondly, the regime published a code of laws which served as a model not only for later Chinese codes but also for those drawn up in Japan and Annam. Finally, it encouraged a major change in the method of recruitment for state service. While the bureaucracy continued to be staffed largely on the basis of family and other connections, the trend during T'ang times was clearly for men increasingly to enter the government through an elaborate system of state-run examinations. Candidates competed in four sessions, the last of which they took in the imperial palace itself. The *chin-shih* degree ("advanced scholar worthy of government appointment") represented the highest possible attainment. By the end of the dynasty, not only were the majority of high officials in the land products of this system, but enormous honor and prestige had come to be attached to successfully passing the various tests.

The military, political, and economic successes of the T'ang era inspired a flowering of Chinese culture characterized by the haunting poetry of Li Po and Tu Fu and Buddhist themes in both painting and sculpture. The perfection of block printing produced the first books probably by the seventh century (although the oldest printed text we have from China dates from 868), almost seven centuries before a similar development in Western Europe. . . .

Song (Sung) Dynasty (960–1270)

With the collapse of the T'ang dynasty, China found herself once again without effective central government. In the north, which soon would fall behind the south in population, cultural attainment, productivity, and wealth, several states known as the Five Dynasties stole the political spotlight from one another in rapid succession over the next fifty years. In the south the situation was worse in one respect yet better in another: there were twice as many states (the so-called Ten Kingdoms), yet their longer histories provided a greater degree of stability to politics and society at large.

Ironically, however, it was a northern regime, the Sung, which restored centralized government to the whole of China in the third quarter of the tenth century. Taking advantage of the achievements of one of the preceding short-lived dynasties in the region (Later Chou), the Sung gradually incorporated the formerly independent states of northern and southern China into their empire. With the aid of a bureaucracy more intricate than that of any previous dynasty, whose members now were drawn predominantly from examination candidates chosen after intense competition, the Sung could provide more uniform, capable, and effective leadership both on the local and national levels. While some criticism was leveled at the examination system for encouraging impracticality and pedantry in successful candidates, the admittedly scanty statistical evidence shows that the system did provide a channel for upward social mobility without producing a self-perpetuating elite. Perhaps thirty percent of all who passed became the first of their families to do so.

In spite of the prosperity which an expanding economy soon brought to Sung China, social problems remained the most pressing domestic concern of the rulers. A monotonously recurrent feature of Chinese life, however, worsened the plight of the peasant. The small farmer could not compete with a growing number of large landowners whose capital resources allowed them not only to acquire more and more land but, through investment in reclamation and irrigation projects and new implements, to derive greater productivity from their estates. . . .

Faced with an ever-present threat from barbarian tribes to the north, the Southern Sung (as the dynasty was now called) became increasingly self-centered and less receptive to alien elements in their society and culture. One example of this changed mood was the rejection of Buddhism as a foreign religion by intellectuals who turned once again to their native Confucianism for in-

MING SEA VOYAGES

Chinese trading ships sailed Asian seas for eight hundred years until the Mongols conquered China and established the Yuan dynasty. The Mongols imposed restrictions on sea trading, and China became very isolated. When the Mongols fell to the Ming dynasty, a forward thinking Ming emperor named Yong'le (1360–1424) encouraged the resumption of sea voyages. Samuel M. Wilson describes here the voyages of Zheng He (Cheng Ho), who was one of the greatest of China's seafaring explorers.

The commander's name was Zheng He (Cheng Ho), the Grand Eunuch of the Three Treasures and the most acclaimed admiral of the Ming Dynasty. He was sailing from the South China Sea across the Indian Ocean, heading for the Persian Gulf and Africa. . . .

As Zheng He pressed westward in 1414, he sent part of the fleet north to Bengal, and there the Chinese travelers saw a wondrous creature. None like it had ever been seen in China, although it was not completely unheard of. In 1225

spiration. But Sung thinkers soon discovered that Confucianism had changed substantially over the previous centuries. As a result, they undertook to re-examine the basic texts and reinterpret their contents. The product of their effort was a synthesis known as Neo-Confucianism, with Chu Hsi as its most notable exponent. By incorporating both Taoist and even some Buddhist elements into his philosophy, he broadened and enriched Confucian concepts to explain man's relationship to the universe. While creating a new orthodoxy, however, Chu Hsi continued to emphasize virtuous behavior and subservience to superiors, two ideas which provided ideological justification for the increasing authoritarianism of Sung politics.

While many people have criticized the Sung dynasty for its failure to preserve the empire's territorial integrity, it is important to note that in many respects Chinese civilization reached its apogee during the Sung centuries. Art, literature, and technology

---

Zhao Rugua, a customs inspector at the city of Quanzhou, had recorded a secondhand description of such a beast in his strange and wonderful *Gazetteer of Foreigners*. He said it had a leopard's hide, a cow's hoofs, a ten-foot-tall body, and a nine-foot neck towering above that. He called it a *zula*, possibly a corruption of *zurafa*, the Arabic word for giraffe.

The giraffe the travelers saw in Bengal was already more than 5,000 miles from home. It had been brought there as a gift from the ruler of the prosperous African city-state of Malindi, one of several trading centers lining the east coast of Africa (Malindi is midway along modern Kenya's coast, three degrees south of the equator). Zheng He's diplomats persuaded the Bengal king to offer the animal as a gift to the Chinese emperor. They also persuaded the Malindi ambassadors to send home for another giraffe. When Zheng He returned to Beijing, he was able to present the emperor with two of the exotic beasts.

Samuel M. Wilson, "The Emperor's Giraffe," *National History*, December 1992, vol. 101, issue 12, p. 22.

(including the priceless invention of printing) all reached a peak of development. . . .

Yuan (Mongol) Dynasty (1279–1368)

The Chinese in the south might have continued to live undisturbed had their rulers not become involved in the problems of the north. Around 1215, the Jürchids appealed for Sung assistance against the Mongols who had already driven them out of Peking. The Sung emperor dispatched infantry in response. Later, after the Mongols had overwhelmed the Jürchids in 1234, the Sung foolishly attempted to reconquer North China. Kublai Khan, who would succeed to the Mongol throne in 1256, promptly launched an invasion of the south. The fighting dragged on for decades before the relentless steppe warriors finally subdued the region in 1279. For the first time the whole of China was ruled by nomads who had not been previously Sinicized and who, despite adopting Chinese institutions and techniques and using Chinese to help administer the country, always remained totally alien.

As the new rulers of China, the Mongols faced the task of administering not only a vast and heavily-populated country but also one with cultural and institutional features at total variance with their own. Accustomed to ruling from the saddle over a relatively primitive and tribally-organized society, what were the Mongols to do with China? At first there was some support for destroying Chinese society, annihilating most of the population, and turning the land into a gigantic pasturage more suited to the nomadic Mongol lifestyle. But the conquerors soon perceived the advisability of leaving the Chinese and their system basically intact to exploit the country more effectively. Thus, the Mongols established an administrative apparatus essentially similar to that which the Chinese had developed. While filling lower-level posts largely with Chinese, the Mongols nevertheless kept all high offices and other important positions for themselves. Furthermore, they tended to make greater use of non–degree holding personnel and foreigners (recall the career of Marco Polo, the Venetian traveler) rather than members of the Chinese elite whom they trusted very little.

The ruling Mongol minority sought to avoid assimilation by clearly relegating the Chinese to secondary social positions. Yet, Kublai Khan himself, greatly influenced by Chinese advisers, ruled as much like a Chinese emperor as a traditional Mongol chieftain. He dutifully performed the Confucian imperial rites, took a Chinese name for his dynasty (Yüan), and even reinstituted the examination system, although examinations were held only once until late in the dynasty. . . .

Ming Dynasty (1368–1644)

Chu Yüan-chang, the leader of the successful revolt against the Mongols, stemmed from humble origins. In fact, he was the first peasant to establish a dynasty (the Ming) in a millenium and a half. His education was informal, which perhaps contributed to his lifelong scorn for intellectuals, yet he had enormous organizational skills and proved astute enough to see the value of recruiting some learned men to assist in administering the territories that he conquered and the state that he would ultimately rule. A man who knew how to handle other men, his harsh and autocratic character had an indelible effect on the dynasty which he founded.

Despotism, in fact, became one of the hallmarks of Ming rule. It resulted in part from new institutional arrangements inaugurated at the very beginning of the dynasty by which emperors exercised enormous and direct responsibility for everyday decisions. It also resulted from the tradition of terrorism, surveillance, and frequent purges which the first emperor established. . . .

For two centuries Ming China thrived. Then by the early part of the 1600s a number of developments began to disrupt the normal workings of government and society. First, there was a growing failure of leadership. Factionalism and intense bureaucratic partisanship, the enormous expansion of eunuch power, and the indifference of many of the emperors made misgovernment an inevitability. Second, China lost both Annam and Burma as a result of uprisings in these tributary states, while two Japanese invasions of Korea, although repulsed by Chinese troops, placed a heavy burden on the imperial treasury. So too did attacks from the north by Mongols and raids all along the China coast by Japanese pirates and Chinese outlaws. Third, the perennial problem of creeping landlordism, particularly in the Yangtze area and the south, led to a considerable number of peasant revolts. Fourth, a doubling of the population caused pressure on the empire's land resources that could not be eased by the repopulation of the formerly devastated northern regions. Finally, increasing governmental incompetence, corruption, arbitrariness, and insensitivity served to alienate most Chinese intellectuals. The growing power of the eunuchs, whose number reached about 100,000, was especially abhorrent to the bureaucratic class.

Ch'ing (Qing) Dynasty–Manchus (1644–1911)

For several generations during the late sixteenth and early seventeenth centuries, a tribe of barbarians known as the Manchus was quietly becoming a unified military power in the southern part of Manchuria. Through diplomacy and conquest a young Manchu chieftain named Nurhachi slowly brought the clans together under his leadership. By the time he was ready to challenge Ming rule over China, Nurhachi's Manchus were already imbued with Chinese culture, had developed Chinese-inspired administrative practices and institutions, and enjoyed the support of large numbers of Chinese farmers who had settled beyond the Great Wall and Chinese officials who had defected from the Ming. . . .

In the 1640s, with the Ming beset by massive internal rebellion, the opportunity came for which the Manchus had waited patiently. In the face of little opposition, they took Peking in 1644 and then swept through the rest of the country. Ming loyalists continued to hold out in remoter areas of the south (especially Taiwan), but eventually they too were destroyed.

Paradoxically, imperial China reached the zenith and the nadir of her development while ruled by the Manchus, who adopted the dynastic title of Ch'ing [Qing]. Under three emperors (K'ang-hsi, Yung-cheng, and Ch'ien-lung), who must rank with the greatest ever to hold that position during China's extensive history, the empire enjoyed extraordinarily long (1661–1796) and dynamic leadership. The results were impressive. On the domestic scene, peace and stability provided the background for such prosperity that under the Ch'ien-lung Emperor taxes were canceled on several occasions. Trade continued to expand throughout the period and handicraft industries proved enormously productive in both quantity and range of commodities. Internationally, the Manchus were especially successful. Brilliant military campaigns extended the empire to Mongolia, much of Central Asia, and Tibet. In the south, Burma, Annam, and Nepal fell under Chinese domination as well.

To ensure the success of their dynasty, the Manchus sought to become "more Chinese than the Chinese." They made few changes in the Ming administrative system (except to balance Chinese officials with Manchus as a controlling mechanism) and, perhaps more importantly, passed themselves off as protectors of Chinese civilization.

The Great Wall of China

By Luo Zhewen

The Great Wall of China is one of the world's most impressive human constructions. In the following commentary, Luo Zhewen explains what the Great Wall means in Chinese civilization. He notes that the Wall has been under construction for two thousand years. Much more than a form of military defense, the Wall also played a role in communications and contributed to economic development and cultural exchange. To this day, the Great Wall is the foremost symbol of China. Luo Zhewen is a lecturer and formerly the expert on architecture at the State Bureau of Cultural Relics and Museum in Beijing, China.

For centuries the Great Wall of China has been one of the wonders of the ancient world.

'There is no good man who has not been to the Great Wall' is a Chinese saying that has come to be used in praise of this great work of architecture not only by all the Chinese people, but also by foreign friends, experts and travellers.

The name of the Great Wall in Chinese is 'The Ten Thousand *li* Wall' (a *li* is a Chinese mile, about one third of an English mile) but it is actually far more than ten thousand *li* long. If we take the length of the Wall as first constructed and add on all the parts built by later dynasties, it is over 100,000 *li*. The scale of construction is without parallel, not only in China but anywhere in the world.

The Great Wall was not simply a defensive wall, nor was it merely a territorial boundary; it was an engineering feat combining defence, communications and other aspects, beacon towers and fortresses. Its many fortified gates, over 1000 castles and more than 10,000 beacons scattered within and without the Wall proper seem to fill the northern half of China. It was extended and restored according to the political and military requirements of each dynasty, whether their capitals were situated north, south, east or west. Today the Great Wall is everchanging; passing over high mountain peaks, snaking across empty grassland plains or crossing the Gobi desert, rising and falling, twisting and dancing.

A Long History

The construction of the Great Wall began in the 3rd century BC. It is by no means the oldest building of the ancient world but it has been constantly under construction for 2000 years, something that cannot be said of any other building in the world.

The history of the Great Wall is generally divided into two stages. The first stage is prior to the reign of the First Emperor of the Qin (who took power in 217 BC) and this is the Wall of the Spring and Autumn Period (770–476 BC) and the Warring States (476–221 BC), a period of China's history when many local rulers were fighting each other for power. The State of Chu was the first to build a wall in the 7th century BC, then the states of Qi, Zhongshan, Wei, Zheng, Han, Qin, Yan and Zhao all built walls of varying lengths. Some were less than 1000 *li*, some several 1000 *li* long.

The second period of the Wall's history dates from 217 BC when the Qin emperor unified the country, and in this phase, over 10 dynasties including the Qin, Han, Northern and Eastern Wei, Northern Qi, Northern Zhou, Sui, Liao, Jin, Yuan and Ming carried out building work on the Wall. The greatest periods of construction were during the Qin, Han, Jin and Ming. Work on the Wall under the first Qin emperor extended it to over 10,000 *li* so it only acquired its name of the 'Ten Thousand *li* Wall' from that period. The Han wall extended from the west bank of the Yellow River to the interior of Xingiang province, and an outer wall was further constructed in the northern part; the full extent of both walls being over 20,000 *li* or 10,000 km. Under the Jin, the Wall was extended from Heilongjiang province to the banks of the Yellow River, an extension of some 10,000 *li*. The Ming was the last dynasty to undertake large-scale work on the Wall (some 7300 km.) and techniques were greatly improved. Many important sections were faced with brick to strengthen them. Most of what we see today is the Ming Wall. . . .

Beginning with the Shang and Zhou dynasties 3–4000 years ago, the Yellow River plain and North China saw a succession of

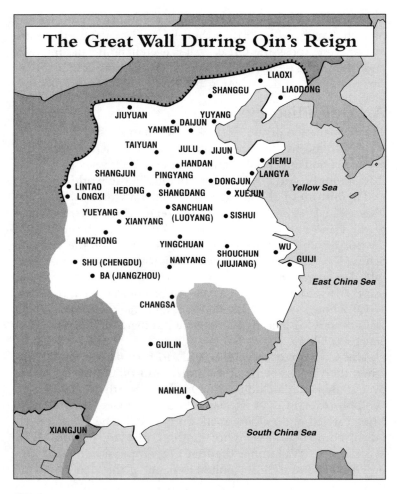

The Great Wall During Qin's Reign

dynasties: Qin, Hen, Sui, Tang, Song, Liao, Jin, Yuan, Ming and Qing. Their capitals and palaces, the heart of their government, were set up in the central Yellow River area, Shaanxi and Shanxi provinces and in Beijing. All the leaders of the minority nationalities that established dynasties came to the central plain in their struggle to gain the imperial position, whether they originated in the mountains of Shaanxi, the high plateau of Mongolia, the pine-covered Liaoning plain or south China. They came to the central Yellow River plain because the land there was fertile, science, technology and culture were highly developed, and all the conditions necessary to support the spiritual and material needs of government were met. No matter from which dynasty or which national minority a new leader came, his first main concern after establishing power was to maintain national security and assure the peaceful livelihood of his subjects. The greatest threats came from the horsemen from the north, north-east and north-west. They came like lightning and left like shooting stars and no generals could prevent them. From the Spring and Autumn and Warring States period (770–217 BC) and through the Qin and Han, the lesson that emerged from all these hundreds of years of experience was that the best form of defence against the sudden attacks of these fast-moving horsemen was to build defensive walls. Thus the construction of the Great Wall began and continued for thousands of years. Whether the ruling group were horsemen from the grasslands of Mongolia or mounted troops from the northern plains like the Northern Wei, Liao and Jin, once they had seized power and established their rule, they in their turn all repaired the Wall to protect their domains. . . .

In its long history of many thousands of years, apart from its straightforward military usefulness, the Great Wall was also a factor in China's foreign relations, in the economic development of the north, in the unification of minority peoples, in cultural exchange and in many other ways. The 2nd century BC saw the establishment of the international trade route known as the 'Silk Road' which relied upon the protection of the Great Wall and its beacon fires to ensure unimpeded movement on the trade route. The arrival of settlers and the produce of the garrison's fields had a great impact on the sparsely populated and economically backward north of China, and most present-day cities along the Great Wall owe their existence to its protection. . . .

The military organization of the Wall was closely linked to its defensive role. Through the experience of thousands of years, it had become a unifying force that went from the centre outwards to the borders. The basic principle underlying the Wall was 'protect the land by dividing; control bit by bit, in sequence'. Taking the Ming wall as an example, the Wall of over 14,000 *li* was divided into twelve garrisons or military areas, each with a General Staff Headquarters as the highest level of authority, directed from the Board [or Ministry] of War. The size of each garrison depended upon the size of the area it had to control, from 10,000 to over 100,000 men (with a total of over a million soldiers). According to local needs, *lu* or circuits were set up below the General Staff Headquarters, led by subordinate officers. A circuit would control some ten gate towers and a stretch of the Wall. . . .

Naturally, the coordination of the garrisons of this 10,000 *li* long Wall with its subordinate walls and territory was not without its problems. Military communication needed to be fast and accurate. Thus the beacon signalling system was perfected by military strategists of over 2000 years ago, using fire and smoke signals. The beacons have been given various names throughout Chinese history: beacon pavilions, smoke mounds or 'wolf smoke towers'. . . .

Structure of the Wall

A great deal of experience in planning, engineering and use of materials was gathered over the thousands of years during which the Wall was constructed, extended and repaired. There are some singular aspects to its construction and engineering. The most important may be summarized in the phrase, 'Build according to the nature of the land; control narrow passes with strategic fortresses'. This is a saying that has been handed down throughout the 2000 years of the Wall's construction. In areas of high mountains and dangerous peaks, the height of the wall is altered according to the lie of the land and the local strategic requirements, making use of precipices or natural cliffs, with gullies and rivers serving as natural protective screens. Strategic gatehouses were situated in the places of greatest threat so that 'one man can hold the gate and ten thousand men cannot get through'.

As the area through which the Wall passes is vast, the geological environment is extremely varied: hence the maxim: 'Build according to the nature of the land and take materials from the land'. . . .

From early on, construction and maintenance were undertaken by local contract and the names of the soldiers who worked on particular sections at particular times can still be seen engraved on stone stelae on the watchtowers.

The Wall Today

The historical usefulness of the Great Wall has completely disappeared today; the battlefields and defensive walls of the past can only serve as an occasional historical lesson. But its magnificence and the solidity of its construction remain as an undying legacy for later generations.

The Opium Wars

By John Newsinger

British intrusion into nineteenth-century China turned violent in the three Opium Wars. Here John Newsinger discusses the events that led up to the wars. Great Britain, dissatisfied with the balance of trade with China, began illegally smuggling opium into China, which dramatically changed the balance of trade in Britain's favor. The opium trade led to huge profits for Britain and drug addiction for many Chinese. When China attempted to stop the smuggling by detaining British merchants and confiscating opium, the British retaliated with military action. China was forced to sign humiliating treaties and to relinquish Chinese territory to the British, most significantly Hong Kong. Newsinger, history lecturer at Bath College in England, is the author of Fenianism in Mid-Victorian Britain *(1994).*

I t is a little known fact that during the reign of Queen Victoria, the British capitalist state was the largest drug pusher the world has ever seen. The smuggling of opium into China was by the 1830s a source of huge profits, played a crucial role in the financing of British rule in India and was the underpinning of British trade throughout the East. . . .

The production of opium in India first came under British control in the course of the eighteenth century. In the 1760s, some one thousand chests of opium (each weighing 140 lbs) were smuggled into China and this figure gradually increased to 4 thousand chests in 1800. By the 1820s the traffic in opium began to increase dramatically with over 12 thousand chests being smuggled into China in 1824, rising to 19 thousand in 1830, 30 thousand in 1835 and to 40 thousand chests (2,500 tons of opium) in 1838. The British energetically encouraged poppy growing, on occasion coercing Indian peasant farmers into going over to the crop. By the end of the 1830s the opium trade was already, and was to remain [in the words of Frederic Wake-

John Newsinger, "Britain's Opium Wars," *Monthly Review*, vol. 49, 1997, p. 35.

man], "the world's most valuable single commodity trade of the nineteenth century."

The opium trade was of vital importance to British imperialism at this time. It was one corner of an Eastern triangular trade that mirrored the eighteenth-century Atlantic slave trade. The smuggling of opium turned a large British trading deficit with China into a substantial surplus, paying for British tea imports from China, for the export of British manufactured goods to India and for a substantial proportion of British administrative costs in India. The opium trade was "the hub of British commerce in the East" [as stated by Jack Gray].

By the end of the 1830s a sixth of British overseas trade was with China and nearly two-thirds of that trade was in opium. . . .

The import of opium into China was, of course, illegal, but the British companies engaged in the trade systematically corrupted or intimidated the Chinese authorities so that it continued with little interruption. Depot ships were anchored off the coast, selling the drug to Chinese smugglers who carried it ashore for distribution. By the 1830s, the scale of the problem forced the Chinese government to respond: the country was being drained of silver to pay for the opium, its administration was being corrupted by foreigners and the extent of addiction (estimates of the number of addicts go as high as 12 million) was seen as a threat to both state and society. In March 1839, the Emperor sent a special Commissioner, Lin Tse-Hsu to Canton to stamp out the trade once and for all.

Lin confined the British merchants in Canton to the European Factories, holding them hostage until the opium held offshore was surrendered. After six weeks, the Superintendent of Trade, Captain Charles Elliot, capitulated and ordered the surrender of 10,000 chests which the Chinese destroyed. This precipitated the First Opium War.

The First Opium War

Once they had been expelled from Canton, the British established themselves on the island of Hong Kong, which they were determined to hold in the face of Chinese hostility. Meanwhile, the British government responded to Chinese actions by demanding compensation for the confiscated opium, the opening of more Chinese ports to trade, the permanent cession of Hong Kong, the legalization of the opium trade, and that China pay the full cost of the British war effort to enforce these demands. A powerful expeditionary force was despatched to bring the Chinese to their senses, first blockading the coast and then proceeding up the Yangtze river to Nanjing. The British had an overwhelming technological superiority that turned every battle into a one-sided massacre. As one British officer observed: "The poor Chinese" had two choices, either they "must submit to be poisoned, or must be massacred by the thousands, for supporting their own laws in their own land."

The British capture of the port of Tin-hai in early October 1841 provides a useful example of the character of the war. The port was bombarded by the *Wellesley* (74 guns), the *Conway* and the *Alligator* (28 guns each), the *Cruiser* and the *Algerine* (18 guns each) and another dozen smaller vessels each carrying ten guns. In nine minutes, they fired fifteen broadsides into the effectively defenseless town before landing troops to storm the ruins. According to one British participant "the crashing of timber, falling houses and groans of men resounded from the shore" and when the smoke cleared "a mass of ruins presented itself to the eye." When the troops landed all they found was "a deserted beach, a few dead bodies, bows and arrows, broken spears and guns. . . ."

The shelling of the town continued as the British troops moved in to rape and pillage. According to the *India Gazette*, "A more complete pillage could not be conceived . . . the plunder only ceased when there was nothing to take or destroy." It was during this war that the Hindi word "lut" entered the English language as the word "loot." The taking of Tin-hai cost the British three men while the number of Chinese killed was over 2,000. Close behind the warships came the opium ships. . . .

The war continued until the Chinese were forced to accept British terms, conceding everything except the legalization of opium. Public opinion in Britain prevented the pressing of this demand, but it was made clear to the Chinese government that the British would not tolerate any further interference with the trade. The most important gain for the British was the cession of Hong Kong. . . .

The Second and Third Opium Wars

The occasion for the outbreak of the Second Opium War was the so-called "Arrow incident" of October 1856. The Chinese authorities arrested a suspected pirate ship, the *Arrow*, that was registered in Hong Kong. The colony's governor, Sir John Bowring, condemned this as an insult to the British flag, demanded the release of the crew and an apology. The Chinese released the crew, but refused to apologize whereupon Bowring, in a fine display of "gunboat diplomacy," ordered the navy to bombard Canton, one of the largest cities in the world. The fact that the *Arrow*'s Hong Kong registration had lapsed at the time of seizure was kept quiet. . . .

The British were joined by the French in the waging of the Second Opium War. Once again the conflict was little more than a succession of technological massacres accompanied by rape and

COMMISSIONER LIN WRITES THE QUEEN

In 1839, the Qing emperor commissioned Lin Zexu (Lin Tse-Hsu) to put an end to the British opium trade into China. Lin tried several tactics, including writing to Queen Victoria. Here are excerpts of Lin's letter to the British monarch.

We are of the opinion that this poisonous article is clandestinely manufactured by artful and depraved people of various tribes under the dominion of your honorable nation. Doubtless you, the honorable sovereign of that nation, have not commanded the manufacture and sale of it. . . . And we have heard that in your honorable nation, too, the people are not permitted to smoke the drug, and that offenders in this particular expose themselves to sure punishment. It is clearly from a knowledge of its injurious effects on man, that you have directed severe prohibitions against it. But in order to remove the source of the evil thoroughly would it not be better to prohibit its sale and manufacture rather than merely prohibit its consumption?

Though not making use of it one's self, to venture nevertheless to manufacture and sell it, and with it to seduce the simple folk of this land, is to seek one's own livelihood by exposing others to death, to seek one's own advantage by other

pillage. The allied forces captured Canton at the end of 1857, but determined to settle with the Chinese government once and for all, Lord Elgin, the British envoy, decided to advance up the Peiho river towards Beijing itself. In May 1858 the Taku forts guarding the mouth of the river were taken and the allied expedition advanced as far as Tientsin where the Chinese capitulated. The Treaty of Tientsin effectively incorporated China into Britain's informal Empire and once the British had withdrawn the Chinese tried to renege on its terms. This provoked the Third Opium War with the British once again taking the Taku forts, but this time proceeding upriver to the military occupation of Beijing in October 1860. Chinese humiliation was complete. . . .

men's injury. Such acts are bitterly abhorrent to the nature of man and are utterly opposed to the ways of heaven. . . .

We now wish to find, in cooperation with your honorable sovereignty, some means of bringing to a perpetual end this opium, so hurtful to mankind: we in this land forbidding the use of it, and you, in the nations of your dominion, forbidding its manufacture. . . . Not only then will the people of this land be relieved from its pernicious influence, but the people of your honorable nation too (for since they make it, how do we know they do not also smoke it?) will, when the manufacture is indeed forbidden, be likewise relieved from the danger of its use. . . .

Let us suppose that foreigners came from another country, and brought opium into England, and seduced the people of your country to smoke it. Would not you, the sovereign of the said country, look upon such a procedure with anger, and in your just indignation endeavor to get rid of it? Now we have always heard that Your Highness possesses a most kind and benevolent heart. Surely then you are incapable of doing or causing to be done unto another that which you should not wish another to do unto you.

Hsin-pao Chang, *Commissioner Lin and the Opium War*. Cambridge, MA: Harvard University Press, 1964, pp. 135, 137.

The British opium trade with China only finally came to an end in 1917. As for Britain's pre-eminent position in China, this began to come under pressure from rival imperialist powers before the end of the century and from Chinese revolutionary nationalism in the early decades of the twentieth century but was only finally eclipsed in the 1930s. What remained, up until 1997, was possession of Hong Kong, the last of the spoils of the Opium Wars.

The Taiping Rebellion

By Jacques Gernet

The Taiping Rebellion against the Qing (Ch'ing) dynasty from 1851 to 1864 was one of the world's most disastrous civil wars. Over 40 million Chinese died before the rebellion was suppressed. The Taiping leader was Hong Xiuquan (Hung Hsiu-ch'uan) (1814–1864), who had been exposed to Christianity in his youth and who came to think of himself as the younger brother of Jesus Christ. In this selection, Jacques Gernet, professor of history at the University of Paris, reviews the rise and fall of the rebellion and the social program instituted by the rebels. The rebels were proto-feminists in that they allowed for certain rights to be accorded to women, and they initiated a sweeping land reform program. Although the Taiping Rebellion failed to overthrow the Qing dynasty, the rebels served as an inspiration for future revolutionaries.

The great rebellion which originated round about 1850 in tropical China had thus had the ground prepared for it by the establishment of secret societies with revolutionary tendencies and a religious tinge. Feelings of hostility towards the Manchus [Qing/Ch'ing rulers] had probably remained alive there since the time of the Southern Ming resistance (1645–61) and the period of secession (1674–81). The speed with which the movement that was to give birth to the T'ai P'ing grew in the province of Kwangsi and spread to the provinces of Kwangtung and of the middle and lower Yangtze is explained not only by poverty and injustice but also by the underground work carried out by the clandestine organizations affiliated to the Society of the Triad (*San-ho-hui*) [precursors of modern-day criminal societies] also known as the Society of Heaven and Earth (*T'ien-ti-hui*).

Jacques Gernet, *A History of Chinese Civilization*, translated by J.R. Foster. New York: Cambridge University Press, 1972. Copyright © 1982 by Cambridge University Press. Reproduced by permission.

Leader of the Rebellion

The man who was to become the head of the great rebel empire of the T'ai P'ing emerged from a despised Chinese minority, the Hakka (K'o-chia), former immigrants into South China. Hung Hsiu-ch'üan [Hong Xiuquan] (1813–64) came from a poor family in eastern Kwangtung, but nevertheless received the rudiments of a classical education and took part, without success, in the official competitions. He was a visionary, predisposed to become one by his temperament, but also perhaps by his origins and the local religious traditions. The reading of tracts handed out by the Protestant missionaries established shortly before in Kwangtung decided him on his vocation of Messiah. The mystical egalitarianism which was to be one of the characteristic features of the T'ai P'ing movement sprang from these first contacts of Hung Hsiu-ch'üan's with the propaganda disseminated by the missions. In 1847 he made the acquaintance of an American missionary called Roberts and started to preach in eastern Kwangtung, a region where the economic depression had made itself felt with particular sharpness since the diversion of trade from Canton to Shanghai which followed the Treaty of Nanking. Emboldened by the success of his preaching, he founded an Association of the Worshippers of God (*Pai-shang-ti-hui*), whose very name recalls the translation adopted by the Protestant missionaries for the name of God (*Shang-ti*). In two or three years he recruited nearly thirty thousand members—unemployed boatmen and carriers in the port of Canton and on the commercial route linking Canton to the valley of the Hsiang in Hunan, miners, charcoal-burners, poor peasants, bandits, and deserters. The society also recruited among the Hakka and the aboriginal inhabitants of Kwangtung and Kwangsi.

Land Distribution and Women

The Worshippers of God, soon known as the T'ai P'ing, first eliminated a rival group in Kwangsi consisting of unions for defence against the banditry which flourished in the region, then merged with the anti-Manchu secret societies. The rebellion started in eastern Kwangsi, in the village of Chin-t'ien-ts'un, in 1850. The T'ai P'ing, who were distinguished by their hair-style—they abandoned the pigtail, the sign of enslavement to the Manchus, and were sometimes to be called 'bandits with long hair', *ch'ang-mao-fei*—destroyed dwellings and proceeded to the

confiscation and sharing out of estates. Distributing land equally
to those of an age to cultivate it, they followed a principle similar to that established by the agrarian laws of the T'ang age and
drew their inspiration from the theory of the draught-board field
(*ching-t'ien*) which figures in the *Chou-li* (*Rites of the Chou*), a work
of dubious authenticity already invoked, in the Han age, by the
usurper Wang Mang and, in the T'ang age, by the empress Wu
Tse-t'ien. Similarly, the organization of individuals and families
in paramilitary groups among the T'ai P'ing was in conformity
with ancient administrative traditions as well as with the framework of the secret societies. Twenty-five families formed a *k'u*
('store'), with its church (*li-pai-t'ang*), five men formed a squad,
five squads a patrol, four patrols a battalion, and so on up to divisions of 2,500 men (corresponding to groups of 13,156 families)
and armies of 125,000 men. Military, religious, and administrative functions were not separated. The T'ai P'ing established a
regime in which no one possessed any property of his own, in
which the individual was very strictly supervised and in which,
after the suppression of all private trade, each person's indispensable needs were satisfied by the collectivity, in which authority
was basically theocratic. All this was not so new as it might seem:
the system had its roots in ancient Chinese political and religious
traditions, in which the myth of a vanished golden age joins up
with the utopia to come. In a very different society and a very
different historical context—the second century A.D.—the Yellow Turbans [peasant rebels suppressed in 184 A.D.] had created a
hierarchical, theocratic society whose object was the establishment of the era of justice and purity bearing the name of Great
Peace (*t'ai-p'ing*), a name taken up again by the Worshippers of
God and called to mind in its own way by the new term of
Kingdom of Heaven (*t'ien-kuo*). Although it is true that Christian influences were perceptible in the T'ai P'ing ('equality is the
ideal of the all-powerful God who has sent Hung Hsiu-ch'üan
to save the world'), and although its adherents were obliged to attend weekly religious services, other influences could also be
noted and the new contributions of Christianity were forced into
a typically Chinese mould. When Hung Hsiu-ch'üan, who governed by divine inspiration, proclaimed himself to be the younger
brother of Jesus Christ, he was only following in the footsteps of
other rebel leaders and usurpers who had been regarded as rein-
carnations of Maitreya, the saviour Buddha. Buddhism, Taoism,

and the classical traditions of the Meng-tzu and the *Chou-li* all made their mark on the T'ai P'ing movement, and the Christian missionaries were struck by the profoundly heterodox aspects of the Christianity professed by these rebels with long hair.

The movement was not only egalitarian and revolutionary, but also puritan and feminist. It condemned concubinage and the practice—which had spread since the Sung age—of bandaging little girls' feet. It aimed at the absolute equality of the sexes in work and war. Women received equal shares of land with the men and formed exclusively female armies. The T'ai P'ing prohibited all useless luxury and forbade gambling for money, alcohol, tobacco and opium. But these puritan—and also iconoclastic—tendencies, which followed the same direction as the propaganda of the Protestant missionaries, were not a radical novelty. The rebellion led by Chang Hsien-chung (1604–47) at the end of the Ming period had also been animated by a destructive rage which attacked luxury goods and the rich. Chang Hsien-chung, too, had created female armies (*p'o-tzu chün*).

Rise and Fall of the Rebellion

In 1851 Hung Hsiu-ch'üan founded the Kingdom of the Heaven of the Great Peace and proclaimed himself King of Heaven (*t'ien-wang*). He conferred this same title of King on his ministers and army commanders: deputy King (*i-wang*) and Kings of the east, west, south, and north. . . .

In 1852 the T'ai P'ing occupied north-eastern Kwangsi (Kweilin area) and south-western Hunan and then advanced towards Ch'ang-sha and the towns on the middle Yangtze (Yüeh-yang, Han-yang), reaching the areas to the south-west of Nanking (Chiu-chiang in Kiangsi, An-ch'ing in Anhwei). The following year they captured Nanking, which they christened Capital of Heaven (*t'ien-ching*). Nanking was to remain the political and administrative centre of the *T'ai P'ing t'ien-kuo* until its fall in 1864. Then came the conquest of the lower Yangtze (Chen-chiang and Yangchow), where they cut communications on the Imperial Canal. In 1853–54 the new empire spread towards the north and west. The T'ai P'ing armies even ventured into the Tientsin area, threatening Peking, but were forced to retreat by cold and hunger; they were defeated in Shantung in 1854. However, the gains of territory in the whole Yangtze valley remained substantial.

In the face of this sudden and triumphant expansion by the rebels the Ch'ing government was at first at a complete loss. The Banners [Qing/Ch'ing military units] were powerless to halt the wave of insurgents and in 1856 the government armies, led by Hsiang Jung, suffered a decisive defeat. The inflow of taxes dropped steeply and transport was disorganized as a result of the halting of traffic on the Yangtze and of the loss of the empire's richest territories. In 1855 there were big floods on the Yellow River, the course of which moved from the south to the north of the Shantung peninsula and was not stabilized until 1870. However, after the first few years of panic and powerlessness the defence was organized effectively, not under the guidance of the central government but on the initiative of the Chinese provincial administrations and the lettered class, which felt directly threatened by a rebellion that attacked the established order and all traditions. New leaders appeared and new, locally recruited armies were formed, sometimes with the financial help of rich merchants. In the west there was the army of the Hsiang, the literary name for Hunan, under the energetic leadership of the Hunanese Tseng Kuo-fan (1811–72), who created a navy for operations on the Yangtze, obtained the moral and material help of the Chinese upper classes and financed the war by issues of paper money and by the new internal toll on commercial traffic, the *lichin*, instituted by the Ch'ing in 1853. This army recaptured Wu-ch'ang, on the right bank of the Yangtze, in 1854, reached Chen-chiang four years later, advanced to Chiu-chiang and threatened Nanking. But the systematic reconquest began only in 1860, with the three armies of Tseng Kuo-fan, Tso Tsung-t'ang (1812–85), another Hunanese (this was the army of Ch'u, the name of the ancient kingdom of the middle Yangtze), and Li Hung-chang (1823–1901), a native of Ho-fei in central An-hwei (army of the Huai).

However, the T'ai P'ing strove to modernize their armies and to reorganize their administration at the instigation of Hung Jen-kan (1822–64), the King of Heaven's cousin, who had received a Western education in Hong Kong and Shanghai and in 1859 published a political treatise (the *Tzu-cheng hsin-p'ien*) in which he advocated the adoption of American political institutions, the creation of railways and of mining and industrial enterprises, the establishment of banks, and the development of science and technology. But the *T'ai P'ing t'ien-kuo* was weakened by internal dissensions among its leaders which were only to grow worse with time. The distribution of land provoked the hostility of the middling and small landowners. The leaders did not respect the rules of austerity imposed on the generality of their followers, but on the contrary lived in luxury. The war and the frequent moves caused the modernization programme to remain a dead letter. The plans for building steamships, railways, and factories had to be abandoned. On the military plane, the T'ai P'ing had advanced too rapidly along the Yangtze valley and had neglected to gain a solid footing in the depths of the countryside. They did not try until 1856 to make an alliance with the Nien, another set of insurgents in North China, and refrained from occupying the Shanghai region in order not to upset the Western powers, whose support they hoped for in vain. Finally, they had no cavalry, a deficiency which robbed them of the ability to manoeuvre quickly. In 1862 the Westerners, who until then had preserved an attitude of relative neutrality, decided to support the Ch'ing, since they felt their interests threatened by the advance of the T'ai P'ing on Shanghai. A corps of mercenaries was formed which was to fight alongside the Chinese troops under the command of the famous British soldier C.J. Gordon (1833–85), the man who was later to meet his death at Khartoum.

In 1864 Tso Tsung-t'ang recaptured Hangchow and started to besiege Nanking. Nanking was taken and the King of Heaven poisoned himself. However, the fighting was to continue against certain elements of the T'ai P'ing armies in Fukien for another two years.

China Loses Territory to Foreign Powers

By J.A.G. Roberts

Defeat at the hands of the British in the Opium Wars (1839–1842, 1856–1860) deeply concerned many Chinese, so they initiated a Self-Strengthening Movement to resist foreign domination. Creating a stronger military was part of this self-strengthening effort. The improved Chinese military quickly had opportunities to test itself. China engaged in sporadic military conflict with France between 1883 and 1885. In the Treaty of Tianjin (1885), China was forced to recognize French control of Vietnam, which had been a Chinese tributary state, and to give economic concessions to France.

China's biggest territorial loss was Korea to Japan in the Sino-Japanese War (1894–1895), described in this selection by J.A.G. Roberts. The Korean government was divided, with some members aligning with China and others with Japan. The assassination of a Korean leader in 1894 led to military intrusion by an increasingly expansionistic Japan. China responded and was easily defeated by the Japanese. Roberts is principal lecturer at the University of Huddersfield in England and author of several books on China.

China's most important and most regular tributary relationship was with Korea. Korea, like Japan, had adopted a policy of international seclusion, but this policy came under threat after Japan had been 'opened' by the United States in 1853. From 1867 the Zongli Yamen [Chinese office handling foreign relations] began to suggest to the Korean court that resistance was not practical and that she [Korea] would be advised to open her ports voluntarily. As a consequence, in 1876 Korea signed an unequal treaty with Japan. From 1879 [military leader] Li Hongzhang took charge of Chinese relations with Korea, and it was with his encouragement that Korea signed a treaty with the United States, thus denying Japan exclusive access. He also secured a commercial treaty and dispatched a young soldier, Yuan Shikai, to create a modern Korean army. In the meantime Japan had also become involved in Korean internal affairs, for the most part encouraging the modernizing faction at court, whereas Chinese support went to the more conservative members. In 1884, while China was involved in war with France, pro-Japanese Koreans headed by Kim Ok-kyun attempted a coup, which failed. This prompted China and Japan to conclude the Tianjin Convention, under which the two countries agreed to withdraw their troops from Korea, to cease training the Korean army and to forewarn the other party of any intention to send troops to Korea. In effect China surrendered her claim to exclusive suzerainty in Korea, which now had the status of a co-protectorate of the two countries.

This compromise survived until 1894, when two events occurred. In March Kim Ok-kyun, the leader of the pro-Japanese group, was murdered in Shanghai by the son of a victim of the 1884 coup. His body was returned to Korea in a Chinese warship, an arrangement which was found offensive by the increasingly vociferous proponents of expansionism in Japan. Meanwhile the threat of a popular movement, the Tonghak insurrection, led the Korean government to appeal to China for assistance. These events gave Japan a pretext for sending troops to Korea. Li Hongzhang attempted to negotiate a settlement, but when the Japanese navy sank the *Kowshing*, a Chinese troopship bringing reinforcements to Korea, war became inevitable.

Despite expectations of a Chinese victory, the contest was brief and one-sided. On land, units from Li Hongzhang's Huai army were defeated at Pyongyang. In September 1894, 12 ships from Li Hongzhang's Beiyang fleet engaged 12 Japanese warships off the mouth of the Yalu river. Four Chinese ships were incapacitated and the remainder took refuge at Weihaiwei, where they were later destroyed. These defeats ruthlessly exposed the limitations of military self-strengthening. China was forced to accept the humiliating terms of the Treaty of Shimonoseki [1895], under which China recognized the independence of Korea and ceded Taiwan, the Penghu or Pescadores islands, and the Liaodong peninsula in southern Manchuria to Japan. Japan also acquired unequal treaty rights in China, and these were supplemented by the right to establish industry in the treaty ports, a right which, by the most-favoured nation principle, devolved to the other treaty powers.

The Qing Emperor Attempts Reform

By Ranbir Vohra

The Opium Wars and Taiping Rebellion seriously weakened the Qing dynasty in the nineteenth century. Between 1895 and 1898, several European powers and Japan demanded concessions in both trade and territory. The Self Strengthening Movement designed to improve China's economic and military capabilities seemed to have failed, and it appeared that China would be divided among the foreign intruders. In the summer of 1898, the Qing emperor Guangxu (1871–1908) issued a number of sweeping reforms known in the West as the 100 Days of Reform. The emperor hoped to transform China's government into a constitutional monarchy. Although the reforms would not have fundamentally altered the whole of Chinese society, the proposed political changes were too much for the conservative ruling class led by Empress Dowager Cixi. She had the emperor put under house arrest and countermanded his reforms. He died still under arrest in 1908, and many scholars believe that Cixi arranged for the emperor to be murdered. She died very shortly after Guangxu died but not before she had chosen the next, and last, Qing emperor, two-year-old Pu Yi (1906–1967).

Ranbir Vohra describes the exciting days of reform and the betrayal that led to the emperor's downfall. Vohra is Dana Professor of Political Science Emeritus at Trinity College and author of many books, including China's Path to Modernization, *from which this selection is taken.*

B y the end of 1898 it appeared that China was about to be dismembered. Even though this did not happen, it was clear that China's sovereignty had been seriously impaired. A helpless, impotent Manchu [Qing] government had allowed the foreigners to slice the country into spheres of influence. The foreign missionaries, who had entered the interior of China propagating a foreign religion and spreading foreign ideas,

Ranbir Vohra, *China's Path to Modernization: A Historical Review from 1800 to the Present*. Upper Saddle River, NJ: Prentice-Hall, 2000. Copyright © 2000 by Prentice-Hall. Reproduced by permission.

were now joined by their compatriots, who were going to invest capital to exploit China's natural wealth, administer and control China's railroads, and sail their commercial vessels in all the major waterways of China. They were all protected, of course, by extraterritoriality and consular gunboats.

The only country that did not participate in the looting of China was the United States; it was busy in 1898 conquering the Philippines. Only one country, Italy, was refused a concession when it joined the scramble and, in 1899, asked for port facilities in Zhejiang.

Shocked by these events, many Chinese, including some who had attacked Kang You-wei [an advocate of constitutional monarchy] for his radical ideas, now agreed that only major political and institutional changes could save China. From 1895 there was significant open public discussion of national issues. . . .

Societies promoting the study of ways and means to strengthen the nation (qiang-xue hui) that had been proscribed in 1896 were reestablished by reform-minded scholars in various provinces, now often with government approval. For the first time privately published periodicals appeared within China (a dozen or so Chinese-language newspapers and periodicals already existed in the treaty ports, run by Chinese businesspersons or missionaries) and began to circulate new ideas. Interestingly provincial governors general often financed these activities. By 1901 there were about 120 newspapers and periodicals.

Even the young Guang-xu emperor had become interested in learning more about world affairs. When he reached the age of majority in 1889, the autocratic empress dowager [Ci-xi] had to hand over the reins of power to him. In fact she still wielded enormous influence because the emperor was her "son" through adoption, had to refer to her as his Imperial Father, and could not go against her wishes. She had also forced him to marry her niece. Moreover, Ci-xi commanded the loyalty of a large number of bureaucrats who owed their position to her patronage. . . .

The emperor's faction came to be associated with reform and Ci-xi's with conservatism.

The most ardent and active reformers were Kang You-wei, Liang Qi-chao, and Tan Si-tong. They were helped, of course, by the writings and ideas of many other like-minded Chinese scholars like Yan Fu, and by the activities of missionaries like Timothy Richard. . . .

The Year of Great Reforms: 1898

In 1897, when the Germans forcibly occupied Jiaozhou Bay and the powers began to "scramble for concessions," it appeared that Kang You-wei's predictions had proved correct. He had warned in one of his 1895 memorials that the Sino-Japanese War had "opened the door to the partition of China by the powers. . . . The danger facing our country has never been so great as it is today."

Before 1897 ended Kang sent his fifth memorial to the emperor, in which he used harsh language to warn that if reforms were not made, China would disappear as a nation and the emperor and his ministers might not even be able "to live the life of commoners." Kang recommended three plans, the best being that the Guang-xu emperor follow the example of Peter the Great of Russia and the Meiji emperor of Japan to initiate reforms preferably using the Japanese model. . . .

Kang was finally summoned to an audience on June 16, 1898. The meeting was exceptionally long, and Kang is reported to have urged the sympathetic emperor to break through the barrier of conservatism surrounding him by appointing vigorous lower officials to carry out the program and by not throwing open the contents of the program for discussion among the senior officials, "who may refuse to put it into effect."

Before long the emperor also met with Liang and Tan Si-tong. Kang, Liang, and Tan were given posts in Beijing. Although the posts were not senior positions, the incumbents were granted permission to memorialize the emperor directly. On the basis of proposals and memorials submitted by Kang and his colleagues, the emperor issued decree after decree ordering the remaking of China. In 103 days 110 imperial edicts were issued, leading to the term *Hundred Days of Reform*.

The new order envisaged a changed examination system that would deal with practical subjects, subjects of contemporary interest, and economics; a new hierarchical school system that would include Western disciplines along with Chinese subjects; conversion of shrines and temples into schools; sending students abroad for study; encouragement of inventions; encouragement of a free press and freedom of the citizens to address the emperor; encouragement of agriculture, industry, and commerce by the establishment of specialized bureaus, specialized schools, trade journals, and chambers of commerce; government sponsorship of railroads and mining; inauguration of a nationwide postal service; rationalization and simplification of the bureaucracy and abolition of sinecure posts; centralization of the fiscal system; modernization and enlargement of the land and naval forces and standardization of the defense industry; and abolition of state allowances for Manchu bannermen.

These reforms covered almost every aspect of China's political, economic, military, educational, and cultural life; if carried out they would have radically changed China. Kang also urged that a constitutional monarchy be established and a national assembly convened, but the emperor did not issue a decree on that subject....

The Emperor Betrayed

The emperor, aware of the danger he was in, accepted Kang's advice that he seek the active support of Yuan Shi-kai, the head of the New Army (with perhaps the best troops available in the country), which was quartered in the Metropolitan province (Zhili province). The easiest way to neutralize Ci-xi was to have Yuan eliminate Ronglu, her close confidant and trusted lieutenant. Ci-xi had arranged to have Ronglu posted as governor general of Zhili and commander of the Northern Armies, which included Yuan's force. The emperor summoned Yuan to an audience on September 16 and promoted him to the honorary rank of vice-president of one of the six boards and placed him in charge of army training. On the eighteenth Tan Si-tong called on Yuan, informed him of the threat to Emperor Guang-xi, and asked him to join the plot against Ci-xi to save His Majesty. Yuan is reported to have said that "killing Ronglu would be as easy as killing a dog."

But Yuan betrayed the plot to Ronglu, who warned the empress dowager. Ci-xi acted swiftly. In a countercoup she seized the emperor on September 21, 1898, and put him under house arrest. An edict was issued in the emperor's name in which he said that Her Majesty had graciously answered his prayer and "condescended ... to administer the government." The emperor, who spent the rest of his days in close confinement, never forgave Yuan Shi-kai for having betrayed him, and it is said that his last words to his brothers before he died were that they should take revenge on the traitor. Thus ended the great promise of a China revolutionized by imperial fiat.

Warned by the emperor, Kang You-wei and Liang Qi-chao escaped, Kang to Hong Kong and Liang to Japan, but Tan Si-tong refused to flee the country and, along with five others, was executed. For four days, until the twenty-fifth, Tan calmly waited for his arrest, telling his friends who recommended escape that without shedding blood there was no hope for a new China. The Six Martyrs of the reform movement of 1898 were executed on the twenty-eighth; many other supporters of the movement were imprisoned or dismissed from office. . . .

The young, inexperienced emperor and his equally young, in-experienced and idealistic advisors did not realize until it was too late that the supposedly all-powerful emperor of China in fact was severely limited in his exercise of power. The emperor's power was circumscribed by traditional ideology and traditional bureaucratic practices. When Guang-xu stepped out of the lim-its set by tradition, he found himself truly powerless. The extra-ordinary influence wielded by the empress dowager only added to his troubles.

The Boxer Rebellion

By Henrietta Harrison

The Boxer Rebellion broke out in the waning days of the Qing dynasty as a direct response to China's humiliation at the hands of foreign powers. At the time, western nations and Japan were carving up China into spheres of influence. Secret societies emerged to oppose Christian and western influences. The most famous of these societies was called the Boxers because its members performed exercises that resembled shadowboxing. The Boxers were nationalistic, superstitious, and violent. Foreigners—especially missionaries and their Chinese converts to Christianity—became targets of the Boxers. By the time the rebellion was suppressed in 1900 by a force of over twenty thousand troops sent by western nations and Japan, 231 foreigners had been murdered.

Henrietta Harrison describes the complexity of the rebellion from the viewpoint of Liu Dapeng, an ordinary Chinese citizen in Shanxi province. Like many Chinese, Liu Dapeng approved of the Boxers' loyalty to China but disapproved of the violence they perpetrated. Harrison is a lecturer in Chinese at the University of Leeds and author of The Making of the Republican Citizen: Political Ceremonies and Symbols in China, 1911–1929.

[I n 1900] Liu Dapeng, a tutor and diarist, stood at the door of his family home in the village of Chiqiao in Shanxi province and watched an army of a thousand Boxers pass through. . . .

Liu's attitude to the Boxers was divided. On the one hand he approved of their loyalty to the Qing dynasty and their opposition to the expansion of foreign power in China. He was particularly supportive of their campaign against the local Catholics, whom he perceived as having sold out to the foreigners. On the other hand, he was dubious about the movement's religious ele-

Henrietta Harrison, "Justice on Behalf of Heaven," *History Today*, vol. 50, September 2000, p. 44.

ments and particularly concerned about the threat they posed to law and order. While he approved of the provincial governor's efforts to force Catholics to renounce their religion, he found it hard to condone the murder of travellers suspected of poisoning wells, let alone pitched battles between Catholic villages and Boxer forces. Liu's feelings, in this respect, were typical of the time and were shared across a wide social spectrum. Indeed, it was just such conflicting attitudes at court that allowed the Boxer movement to spread on such a wide scale. Although events in the northern coastal province of Shandong where the Boxer movement originated are better known, some of the worst violence in the uprising took place in the adjoining Shanxi province, witnessed by Liu.

Opposition to Foreign Powers

The Boxers' opposition to the foreign powers and especially to Christianity struck a chord with many Chinese and drew widespread support. China's defeat by Japan in the war over Korea in 1894 [Sino-Japanese War, 1894–1895] was a turning point in perceptions of the foreign threat. The country's perception of itself as the Middle Kingdom, a central realm of civilisation surrounded by tributary states, and by savages and barbarians beyond that, had been affirmed by Korea, which had conducted an elaborate tributary relationship with China. The loss of Korea, moreover, brought with it humiliating defeat by the Japanese, hitherto often dismissively referred to as 'dwarf pirates'. In the Treaty of Shimonoseki, which concluded the war, China not only agreed to Korean independence, but ceded Taiwan to Japan and gave the Japanese the same treaty rights as those of Westerners. These were the events that roused Sun Yat-sen, later China's first President, to plan his first revolutionary uprising. But it was not only members of China's tiny reformist elite who were concerned at this outcome. The news was carried across the country and was talked about by the farmers in Chiqiao village, all of whom, Liu reported, opposed the terms of the treaty. . . .

Popular opposition to foreign power was confirmed in Shanxi when news came through in the summer of 1900 that the government had declared war on the foreign powers. Liu heard that governors had been ordered to kill collaborators, that is to say Christians, and to arrest any foreigners and execute them if they planned to make trouble or plotted with the Christians. Shanxi's governor, Yu Xian, was said to be delighted at the news and immediately sent soldiers to round up those foreigners residing in the province and bring them to the provincial capital. Less than a month later some forty unfortunate foreigners were formally executed outside the provincial government building. The Chinese leaders of the Catholic community were ordered to renounce their faith and one who refused was executed. It was thus clear that the government declaration of war on the foreign powers included not only foreign civilians but also Catholic villagers. When the Boxers marched through the countryside carrying banners that said 'Restore the Qing! Destroy the foreign!' their claims that they were loyal forces obeying the orders of the dynasty were hard to deny.

Catholics were seen as potential collaborators in a war with the foreign powers because Christianity had been introduced into China by foreign missionaries. Indeed the right for Christian missionaries to reside in the interior had repeatedly been the object of treaty negotiations between the Qing dynasty and the foreign powers. In Shanxi, the Protestant missionaries had only a handful of converts, but Catholicism was firmly rooted in many rural areas and had been widespread since the eighteenth century. The heart of the problem lay in the contradictions between Christianity and the belief system that underlay the structures of the state. In the villages—where the Boxers operated—the problems of integrating Christianity in the imperial state were focused around the issue of temple festivals and opera performances. Temple festivals were funded by contributions from all members of the local community. In addition to a market they included sacrifices to the deity in whose honour the festival was held and often theatrical performances on a stage facing the temple. Wealthy villages would hire a travelling opera company who would perform for three to five days. Poorer villages might only have a puppet theatre for a single day. The festival performances were intended for the deity but were also a source of entertainment. Friends and relations came from miles around to see the operas, meet and chat, while the market drew large crowds. The funds raised to pay for the opera, meanwhile, also provided a working budget for such village level local government as existed. They might, for example, be used to pay for the dredging of dikes for a communal irrigation system or a law suit against a neighbouring village. Christians, however, refused to pay the levies on the grounds that they would be used to support idolatrous practices. By refusing to contribute to the festivals, Shanxi Catholics were excluding themselves from the local community. . . .

The issue of Catholic refusal to participate in the religious practices of the local community became particularly powerful and problematic in the summer of 1900 because of the fear of drought. Drought was a constant threat to the North China Plain, where farmers rely on rain falling at precisely the right times of year. In Shanxi many remembered with fear the great famine of the 1870s when in Chiqiao one in ten of the population died, and in parts of the south of the province the death toll was worse still. Drought like this was widely seen as divine punishment for immorality and people reacted with ritual and prayer. . . . Catholic refusal to participate in the rituals needed to save the local community from famine accentuated an already problematic relationship. . . .

Boxers as Threat to Law and Order

However, the people of Chiqiao village, which had no Catholic families at all, nevertheless fled in panic when they heard the Boxers were approaching the village. Doubts lingered about the beliefs and rituals of the Boxers, and about their violence. People expected that boxing, or martial arts, techniques would be learned from a teacher over many years, but these were mostly young boys with hardly any training. Liu Dapeng went to see them practising at a large temple near Chiqiao. They set up sticks of incense and kowtowed to them. Then they stood facing south-east, put their hands in a certain position and recited an invocation to several deities. Immediately they fell on the floor, as if asleep. Then, as the crowds of spectators gathered, their hands and feet began to move and slowly they stood up and began a kind of dance sometimes with weapons, all the time keeping their eyes closed. Although their expressions were terrifying, they somehow looked as if they were drunk. After keeping up these strange movements for a while they fell to the ground again, and eventually awoke. Later they said that they did not remember what they had done while they were in the trance. When one of the onlookers asked what would happen if they had to face guns, they replied that Heaven was angry and had sent them as soldiers to warn the people. This was the 'spirit possession' that was central to the Boxer movement. Spirit possession by semi-professional mediums is a feature of Chinese folk-religious practice, but mass spirit possession of this sort was as Liu commented, very strange indeed. . . .

But the strangeness of Boxer claims was not limited to spirit possession. As at other times when drought threatened, bizarre rumours were rife. In Shanxi it was said that the wives of the foreign missionaries stood naked on the roofs of their houses fanning back the winds that would have brought rain. Other rumours concerned the Catholics, who were said to be poisoning village water supplies. Western power, and particularly science, was considered to border on black magic in the eyes of much of the population. The same black magic was also attributed to the Chinese Catholics. Rumours spread through Shanxi that Catholics had painted blood on doorways, and where they had done this the entire family would go mad within seven days. The Boxers claimed to have the power to oppose this Catholic magic and Liu saw people washing the blood off their doors with urine as the Boxers instructed. Strange stories told of full-scale battles between the Catholic and the Boxer magic. In a large town near Chiqiao there was a panic one night that the Catholics had come and many of the townspeople went to guard the city walls. When they were there they heard a huge noise like tens of thousands of people attacking and then suddenly a green hand as big as a cartwheel appeared in the air. The local Boxer leader pointed at it and there was a crash of thunder and rain began to fall. He explained that the green hand had been a form of Catholic magic and he had destroyed it. Outside the city wall the villagers saw the lights, heard strange noises and fled from their homes in panic to hide in the fields. It is clear that such stories were widely believed at the time, and yet there was always an underlying distrust. The next morning, when the villagers cautiously emerged from their hiding places, they realised that there had been no Catholic army and no battle. The fear of drought inevitably gave rise to rumours, but many including Liu were not wholly convinced by the magical claims of the Boxers.

Distrust of the Boxers' spiritual powers was increased by a growing realisation of the threat they posed to law and order. This began with the murder of people accused of poisoning wells. Most of these were not even Catholics, but were accused of being in their pay. Magistrates, unsure of how to respond to the movement, failed to investigate the crimes and Boxer confidence grew. Large groups of men assembled and began to fight their Catholic neighbours. The army of men that Liu saw marching through his village had gone out to a nearby village which had a sizable Catholic population. The Catholics had hired men from another province to protect them and had withdrawn to their solidly-built stone church. The Boxers besieged the church and the battle lasted for six days. More than thirty of the mercenaries were killed before the church fell. A few of the Catholics survived the seige and escaped, but the rest were massacred and the church burned.

Divisions Within Government

Magistrates' failure to act in the face of such disorder was due to the weakness and indecision of the central government, which vacillated between support for the Boxers and fear of the foreign powers. For more than fifty years the foreign threat had been at the centre of factional divisions within the court. At the heart of this debate was the question of whether a modern, well-equipped army or popular feeling should be more important in withstanding the foreign powers. The leaders of the bureaucracy were examined and trained in Confucian thought and for many of them it was an article of faith that victory in battle would be the result of the people's support. On the other side stood a faction, many of whom were drawn from the Manchu ruling ethnic group, who had accepted the strength of the European powers and believed that it was necessary to approach them cautiously until such time as China had built up the technical expertise to face them. The radical Confucians saw the growth of the Boxer movement as a sign that the people were at last aroused to fight the foreigners. Putting their trust in this, they were prepared to overlook the folk-religious aspects of the movement, which were clearly at odds with Confucian rationalism, and also the inevitable threat to law and order that would arise if the people were allowed to bear arms outside state control. With the support of the ruling Empress Dowager the court declared war on the foreign powers. However, the more cautious modernisers, many of whom had power bases in the southern provinces, believed that China was still unable to defeat the foreign powers; the governors general of the southern provinces refused to enter the war. Instead they drew up private agreements with the foreign powers, giving protection to foreigners and Christians in return for a promise that the foreigners would not invade. Although the Confucian radicals had won at court the central government was not strong enough to control the regions. The result was indecision and a series of conflicting orders. The Qing army never really engaged with the foreign troops, but county magistrates dared not arrest the Boxers, and thus appeared to be encouraging the movement to spread.

THE HISTORY OF NATIONS
Chapter 2

Revolution and War: China in the Early Twentieth Century

Sun Yat-sen and the Revolution of 1911

By Leonard H.D. Gordon

Sun Yat-sen is known as the father of modern China because of the significant role he played in organizing a revolution against Qing imperial rule and in establishing the Chinese republic. In the final years of the Qing dynasty, China was losing territory and national autonomy to foreign powers, and the central government was losing control to regional leaders. Although Sun started as a reformer, he became convinced that the only solution to China's political problems was revolution.

Sun formed the revolutionary United League in 1905, and he traveled widely to gather support for his cause. He was raising funds in the United States when the Chinese revolution broke out in 1911. Sun returned to China and became provisional president of the new republic, a position he held for only a few months. Sun turned over the presidency to Yuan Shikai, a powerful military leader, with the provisions that the Qing emperor abdicate and that Yuan promise to support a republican constitution.

Here Leonard H.D. Gordon, professor emeritus of Chinese history at Purdue University, discusses Sun's early years and education, his revolutionary activities, and his political philosophy. Gordon also describes Sun's relations with warlords and Communists and his establishment of the Nationalist Party (Guomindang). Gordon and Sidney H. Chang coauthored All Under Heaven: Sun Yat-sen and His Revolutionary Thought *(1991).*

The history of China is filled with rebellions, uprisings, and foreign invasions. These disturbances often brought new leaders and dynasties to power, but none of them genuinely revolutionized China's government, economy, or society. Revolution as experienced in the West was foreign to traditional China. In the course of its modernization, however, China

Leonard H.D. Gordon, "Sun Yat-sen and His Legacy," *World & I*, vol. 14, September 1999, p. 328. Copyright © 1999 by *World & I*. Reproduced by permission.

underwent two colossal upheavals: the Nationalist revolution of 1911 led by Sun Yat-sen and the Communist revolution of 1949 led by Mao Zedong.

Sun Yat-sen, who emerged as the recognized leader of the 1911 revolution, was intensely nationalistic, visionary, and devoted to his cause. Sun was born during the Qing dynasty (1644–1912), which was dominated by Manchu tribesmen who had invaded China from north of the Great Wall. By the mid-nineteenth century, this dynasty was nearing total collapse. Burdened by resistance to change and weakened by the stubborn and ignorant Empress Dowager Zi Xi (Ts'u-hsi), China faced many social ills—opium smoking, gambling, footbinding of young females, infanticide, and an intransigent and autocratic bureaucracy—all of which aroused a need for drastic reform. Meanwhile, the world was in turmoil from Europe to Asia. Clashing ideologies including capitalism, socialism, imperialism, colonialism, and nationalism—all stirred by rising industrialization and dramatic new forms of communication and transportation—resulted in challenges for which China was unprepared. . . .

Early Years and Education

In some ways, Sun Yat-sen (1866–1925) was an unlikely leader to confront the rapid and dramatic changes of the late nineteenth and early twentieth centuries. Born of peasant background in the small village of Cuiheng (Ts'ui-heng) in southern China, he had no government experience, formal classical education, or official contacts. Unlike his reformist rivals, however, Sun received a Western education in Hawaii and Hong Kong, enabling him to study English, medicine, and Christianity. Sun's first Western experience occurred in 1879 when his mother took him to Hawaii, where he enrolled in an Anglican school.

Four years later he entered Oahu College, an American Congregationalist school. Sun's brother, a successful businessman and landowner in Hawaii, was appalled at his younger brother's serious attitude toward Christianity and wrote to their father, who ordered Sun home "to take this Jesus nonsense out of him" and expressed dismay that he would "take up with the superstition of the foreign devils." Sun was not dissuaded, however, and went to Hong Kong in April 1884 and continued his Western and Christian education. Retaining adherence to Chinese tradition, he entered an arranged marriage with a woman from his home village. In the same year, he was baptized, but his adherence to Christian observance waned as he became more involved in revolutionary activities.

By the age of twenty, Sun became less enamored with some aspects of traditional Chinese beliefs and entertained thoughts about overthrowing the Qing dynasty, ruled by the non-Chinese Manchus. At the same time, he sought a career and decided on medicine (deemed "respectable" in China, it gave him an opportunity to expand his knowledge of Western science). His experiences as a medical student led him to think about the necessity of modernizing China along Western lines, abolishing the practice of opium smoking and other social problems, and improving agricultural techniques. Sun entered the College of Medicine for Chinese in Hong Kong in 1887 and five years later graduated at the top of his class. Since his school was not recognized by the General Medical Council of Great Britain, he could not practice in Hong Kong and moved to Macao, where he opened the China-West Pharmacy.

Sun as Revolutionary

It was in Macao in 1892 and early 1893 that Sun thought seriously about revolutionary activities. In an effort to appeal to a distinguished official, he wrote a lengthy letter to Li Hongzhang in Tianjin proposing the development of new technologies and economic programs and arguing for the importance of commercial expansion for China. Li was preoccupied with the Sino-Japanese War (1894–95) and did not respond. Disappointed, Sun returned to Hawaii, where he established China's first revolutionary organization, the Revive China Society (Xingzhonghui) with twenty members. Once back in China, he began his revolutionary activities with the first of a series of unsuccessful uprisings at Guangzhou (Canton) on October 26, 1895.

In the next sixteen years before the revolution of 1911, Sun frequently went into hiding from the Qing authorities who sought his capture, often going to Japan and Southeast Asia as well as the United States and Europe in pursuit of funding and diplomatic support. In Japan, he changed his name to Nakayama, cut off his queue, wore Western clothing, and grew a mustache to blend into modern Japanese society. Most important was his friendship with the Miyazaki brothers, who helped him financially and introduced him to other progressive-minded Japanese sympathetic to China's revolutionary cause.

Continuing his persistent search for money, he traveled to Hawaii, the United States, and England. On October 1, 1896, he arrived in London, where he renewed his friendship with Dr. James Cantlie, who had been helpful to him while at medical school in Hong Kong. A dramatic and unexpected event took place ten days after his arrival. While on his way to accompany Dr. and Mrs. Cantlie to church, he was "invited" by two strangers into a residence on Portland Place. Once there, he was quickly taken to a third-floor room and imprisoned! He had been kidnapped by the Qing Legation in London. During his house arrest of eleven days, he was able to deliver a message to Cantlie with the help of a sympathetic servant. Failing to gain cooperation from Scotland Yard, Cantlie went to the *London Globe* and publicized the kidnapping, thereby embarrassing the Qing government, which felt compelled to release Sun.

Sun was genuinely frightened for his life during his captivity. He later wrote that he feared his "ankles [would be] crushed in a vise and broken by a hammer, my eyelids cut off, and, finally [I would] be chopped to small fragments, so that none could claim my mortal remains." The significance of this sordid episode was that Sun received worldwide attention and recognition for his revolutionary activity.

Formation of United League

By 1903 his revolutionary objectives expanded beyond toppling the Qing dynasty to include the elimination of all Manchu influence, the establishment of a republic, and the equalization of land ownership. To accomplish these goals, he created the Chinese Revolutionary Army. In this period, he worked closely with Huang Xing in creating a series of revolutionary groups. By 1905, the United League (Tongmenghui) was formed and became the central revolutionary organization, with other groups joining it. Numerous newspapers, journals, magazines, books, and pamphlets soon appeared carrying Sun's revolutionary message.

The primary voice of the United League was its journal, *Minbao*, which promoted revolutionary concepts and criticized nonrevolutionary Chinese reformers and imperial Japanese exploitation of China. For this latter boldness, the journal was banned from Japan. Nevertheless, the United League secretively set up branches in Southeast Asia, the United States, Europe,

Hong Kong, and Singapore. Funding for its activities remained a constant problem. Money came from Chinese businessmen abroad, membership fees, contributions, and shares sold within the organization. These efforts, however, were ancillary to planning and executing major uprisings against the dynasty. Between 1895 and April 27, 1911, ten attempted uprisings failed, and the revolutionary movement appeared to be stalled.

The United League planned to strike at Wuchang in the Yangzi Valley in late October 1911. Before these plans were completed, an accidental explosion took place in the basement of a building in the Russian area of nearby Hankow [in Wuhan, Hubei Province]. When local Manchu police investigated, they discovered a list of revolutionaries in the area. To avoid arrest, the United League had to act quickly. It revolted, overcoming Qing resistance with surprising ease. Near the end of the year, the revolutionaries set up a temporary government at Nanjing. Where, in all of this, was Sun Yat-sen? Not expecting a major uprising to take place, he was in Denver, Colorado, on a fund-raising mission. Knowing past failures, he did not take the news seriously and continued on his voyage to Washington, London, and Paris.

A Republic Is Established

When Sun returned to China, he was made provisional president of the new Republic of China, but he immediately faced a major dilemma. The northern half of China was still controlled by Gen. Yuan Shih-kai and his superior army, which supported the Manchu government. To resolve the conflict, Sun offered the presidency to the general with conditions attached. The emperor would have to abdicate, while Yuan would have to declare a republican government and take an oath to support the constitution prepared by the provisional parliament. After these provisions were implemented, Sun, who took office on January 1, 1912, relinquished his title and duties on April 1. Later in the year, the Tongmenghui absorbed four lesser parties and formed the Nationalist Party (Guomindang), which would carry on Sun's program. When the emperor abdicated in February and his royal entourage retreated behind the walls of the "forbidden city" in Beijing, the Manchu dynasty that had governed China for over 268 years vanished.

During Sun Yat-sen's brief tenure as president, he devoted his attention to serious issues: integrating ethnic minorities, enhancing welfare needs of the poor, promoting women's rights, and opposing the archaic practice of footbinding. He was also concerned about the problems of farmers and the debilitating practice of opium smoking. In addition, he promoted the separation of church and state, a free press, and the use of domestic silk and cloth. Progress on these issues, however, was short-lived. When Yuan ascended to the presidency, he showed no respect for democratic procedures and arrogantly resorted to political chicanery, cajoling, bribery, threats, and assassination to expand his power.

At the beginning of Yuan's presidency, Sun accepted the responsibility of developing a railroad system for China, which he thought was essential for a modern society, and prepared elaborate plans. However, when Song Jiaoren, Sun's close associate in the revolution, was gunned down in cold blood at the railway station in Shanghai and the heavy hand of Yuan Shih-kai was implicated in the plot, Sun was devastated. Joined by Huang Xing, he considered military action against the Yuan government. In May 1913, Sun broke completely from Yuan, and the following January Yuan dismissed the parliament and became virtual dictator of China. The charade of preparing a new constitution in May 1914, making himself "president" for a ten-year term that was "indefinitely renewable," fooled no one. Unsatisfied with being a dictator, Yuan prepared to make himself emperor of China in December 1915. Illness quickly followed. Yuan's death on June 6, 1916, from uremia ended his farcical attempt to reestablish the empire.

Warlords and Communists

During Yuan Shih-kai's reign Sun went to Japan once again and had a falling out with Huang Xing over a change in policy. Sun, who once sought nonviolent means, changed to endorsing a military solution, while Huang, who once sought military means, now turned to diplomacy. After Yuan's death, a series of weak leaders followed, supported by local military commanders, or "warlords." To challenge this despotic and ineffective government in Beijing, Sun set up a rival military government in Guangzhou in September 1917. In real terms, Sun's illegal operation in Guangzhou was in a state of civil war with the internationally recognized government in Beijing. Like the northern government, Sun relied on warlord armies in the south for his military, but the local provincial commander, Chen Jiongming, betrayed

Sun and drove him out of the city, burning Sun's office and papers and forcing him to flee. Stymied by a lack of broad public support, unreliable warlords, rivalries, betrayals, and military failures, Sun spent considerable time writing between 1917 and 1921 on national reconstruction for China and planning for the revitalization of his revolutionary movement.

Unable to gain recognition from the West, Sun looked toward Russian Communists. The Communists had established a radical state, the Soviet Union, and Sun admired their organizational skills and training programs. Seeking assistance, Sun met with a Communist agent, Adolfe Joffe, in January 1923 in Shanghai. In the document they signed, Sun separated his own ideological principles from those of Marxist-Leninist thought, noting that communism and the Soviet system were not compatible with Chinese beliefs. Joffe accepted Sun's caveat, thus establishing the alliance. After Sun's forces drove Chen out of Guangzhou, enabling Sun to return, Sun welcomed another Communist agent, Michael Borodin, who arrived in Guangzhou on October 6 to assist him in streamlining the Nationalist Party into a structured and disciplined organization.

After a failed attempt to seize the Beijing government's customs service, Sun realized that he needed to prepare his own military organization with well-trained officers. In May 1924 Sun opened the Army Officers School, known as the Whampoa Military Academy. His plan was to use graduates of this school in a "northern expedition" that would bring all of China under the leadership of the Nationalist Party. A young supporter trained in the Soviet Union, Chiang Kai-shek, was chosen as commandant of the academy with about five hundred cadets.

In an effort to avoid direct conflict with the Beijing government, Sun attempted a diplomatic tactic. In mid-November 1924, he traveled north via Hong Kong, Shanghai, and Japan. When he reached Tianjin on December 4, 1924, he was quite ill and experiencing severe pain. He proceeded to Beijing and entered the Medical Union College Hospital, where he was diagnosed and treated for cancer of the liver. He was obviously too ill to negotiate a possible unification settlement with Duan Qijui, the provisional head of the Beijing government. Accepting the generosity of a talented diplomat, V.K. Wellington Koo, Sun went to his home and died there on March 12, 1925. In addition to a will leaving his modest possessions to his wife, Sun left another "will," drafted at his request by Wang Jingwei, urging his followers to complete his unfinished revolution.

Sun's *Three People's Principles*

Despite his frequent travels and narrow escapes with his life, Sun spent considerable time writing lengthy treatises that described his program for a democratic, republican form of government. His most important document is *The Three People's Principles* (Sanminzhuyi), which he revised several times and completed in 1924 as a series of public lectures.

The first principle was "Nationalism," under which Sun envisioned a creed to unite divergent groups throughout China and eliminate the influence of the "savage," "barbarous" Manchus. The roots of China's modern nationalism were in response to the unequal treaties, which gave Westerners in China's port cities special privileges over the Chinese. Although Sun condemned the intrusion of all foreigners in China, he favored a conciliatory approach to the Japanese, whom he saw as natural allies because of cultural and racial ties, and individual Westerners, whose science and technology could prove beneficial for modernizing China. Sun believed that nationalism would unify China, which struck him at the time as "a heap of loose sand."

The second principle was "Democracy." Under this principle, Sun's idealism foresaw a blend of selected Western practices and Chinese values. Conscious of China's disorder, he favored a strong government led by a "centralized democracy" in which the state possessed more power than a Western democratic government. While accepting a separation of powers and the three branches of government in the American system—executive, legislative, and judicial—he added two branches from traditional Chinese institutions: the examination yuan, for the selection of superior public servants, and the censorial yuan, to oversee activities of high officials. In the latter, the power of impeachment was the sole function of a separate branch of government.

Although Sun did not adhere to all aspects of the American democratic system, he favored equal opportunity for every Chinese citizen. His concern that the public participate in government is reflected in his acceptance of the rights of election, recall, initiative, and referendum.

The last principle was "Livelihood," under which Sun combined elements of socialism, capitalism, and Chinese traditionalism. This principle was the most controversial and complex of his doctrine. Although it has been translated as "socialism" (shehuizhuyi), it differed from the Marxist view that materialism was the primary motivating force in history and that class struggle between capitalists and the working class was essential to bring about social change. Sun held to the traditional Chinese view that human behavior was based on spiritual values and morality.

Sun on Land Reform

In writing about private capital, state capital, and the equalization of land rights, Sun was influenced by Henry George, an American progressive, and Edward Bellamy, an author critical of monopolistic growth and inequality in the United States. While drawing upon the ideas of these writers, Sun was also influenced by John Stuart Mill and ancient Chinese land policies. In his advocacy of capital regulation, Sun favored placing China's national industries into a "Great Trust" owned by the Chinese people. Management of the industries, he warned, must be in the people's interest lest government become autocratic.

On the equalization of land ownership, Sun proposed a single-tax system similar to that of the Zhou dynasty over two thousand years before. Designed to prevent an excessive accumulation of wealth, the single-tax system stipulated that land values as determined by the landowners be taxed at a universal rate of approximately 1 percent. The land belonging to those who could not pay their taxes would be confiscated and distributed to the landless. This emphasis on rural issues was not appreciated by Chinese Communists, because the Principle of Livelihood did not stress the industrial working class....

Sun and Communism

Sun and his Communist advisers were brought together by necessity and a common disdain for imperialism and colonialism. Although Sun accepted many of their ideas, especially in regard to the structure and organization of the Nationalist Party, there were subtle differences nevertheless. One difference lay in the fact that Sun's land reform focused on the equalization of land ownership with fixed taxation and land value rather than on communalization. Moreover, his industrialization program was based on the acceptance of foreign capital, not class struggle; and although he was concerned about imperialism, he did not equate it with the "evils" of capitalism. Additionally, although he regarded his principles as close to communism in achieving equality in ownership, he saw a difference in the methods applied.

Chinese Communist opinion on Sun's principles, as expressed by Mao Zedong, was skeptical about similarity between the two doctrines. Mao observed with dismay that people's power, the eight-hour working day, and a full-scale agrarian revolution were not in *The Three People's Principles*. While democratic revolution was included, a socialist revolution was omitted. In addition, Mao believed that the principles were inconsistent in theory and practice. Although the Communists saw elements of socialism in Sun's principles and regarded him as having progressive ideas, they—like himself—did not believe he accepted all the concepts of communism.

The Warlord Period

BY DAVID BONAVIA

In 1912, Sun Yat-sen relinquished the presidency of the new Republic of China to Yuan Shikai (1859–1916) with the proviso that Yuan would follow the new Republic's constitution. Yuan, who was a military leader in control of a large region in northern China, tried instead to make himself the emperor of a new dynasty. When Yuan died in 1916, China completely collapsed into an era known as the "warlord" period. The country was divided into a number of regions, each dominated by a military strongman. Journalist David Bonavia describes the emergence of warlords and their precedent in Chinese tradition and history. The warlord period came to an end when Chiang Kai-shek defeated the northern strongmen and united China under a nationalist government in 1926.

Before his death, Bonavia was a contributor to the London Times *and* Far Eastern Economic Review. *He is the author of several books, including* The Chinese, Verdict in Peking, *and* Hong Kong: Living with the Future.

The unwarlike Dr. Sun [Sun Yat-sen] was poorly equipped to handle the process of military centrifugalism which set in after Yuan Shikai's death in 1916. Yuan, who had been made president of the new Republic by the Provisional Parliament, had attempted to have himself enthroned as emperor. The country split up into half a dozen main areas dominated by regional commanders, with hundreds of petty commanders and mere bandits holding out in individual cities or remote areas. These men, the most powerful of whom were called warlords in English, *dujun* or *junfa* in Chinese, were mostly professional soldiers, some trained in modern war colleges with European and Japanese advisers, or bandits who had collected enough followers to wield sufficient military force.

With the formal collapse of the dynasty and the failure of Yuan Shikai to make himself emperor, China entered into the warlord period. Though generally thought to have lasted from 1916 to 1928, in fact it continued, in a residual way, until 1937 and the Japanese invasion. Local and regional commanders gathered their troops around themselves in a system of commander-soldier relationships, which was of considerable strength in that it provided a substitute for the emperor-citizen relationship—the ideological basis of the late empire. The warlords' troops fought—when they did fight—mainly out of loyalty to their commander, and of course for food and loot. Most were mere boys. They were deficient in training, discipline, uniforms, arms, and medical supplies. Their preferred manner of fighting was to shuffle in the general direction of the enemy, loose off a shot or two without aiming, then sit down to await further orders. But they were also capable of ferocity and valour.

A History of War

Modern warlordism was a specific product of the twentieth century, but its roots lie far back in Chinese history. Until the end of the third century BC, China was split into a number of kingdoms, the Warring States, and fiefdoms which expanded to absorb or conquer their neighbours, or suffered eclipse while their ruling families were massacred by victorious enemies.

Even after the unification of China under the first Qin emperor in 221 BC, military revolt and full-scale civil war were only held temporarily in abeyance. The collapse of the Qin dynasty in 210 BC was followed by a fierce war of succession in which the victorious commander, Liu Bang, founded the stable and prosperous Han dynasty. Sometimes starving or oppressed peasants formed themselves into bands with special insignia in their dress—such as the Yellow Turbans in the second century AD. Peasant rebels up until the twentieth century often practised religious or pseudo-religious cults to increase their cohesion and ensure their own victory.

The vast extent of the empire at the height of the Tang dynasty (AD 618–907) led to the creation of military governorships in outlying areas, which gradually won more and more autonomy from the central government—to the point where they could assert their military independence and even threaten the ruling dynasty.

In Chinese historical tradition, war was considered a matter of stratagems, and bluffs, more than a question of slogging it out on the battlefield. The greatest military philosopher of ancient times, Sun Tzu, had declared that 'all war is deception'. Night manoeuvres, surprise attack, treachery, bribery, and shifting alliances—the Chinese commander was admired most if he mastered all these practices and used them to the full before committing his troops to the field of battle. There was little clemency, however, and the losing side were routinely massacred or enslaved. The 'cunning Ulysses' of the Greek Odyssey would have found more to admire in Chinese warfare than the blunt Julius Caesar, who fought Rome's wars with iron discipline and brute strength.

China has its own code of military honour and gallantry, but this system was held in slight esteem by the Confucian scholar-administrators, who despised soldiers and cordially disliked war. By contrast with the European tradition, a young man of the gentry class would not especially consider himself gaining glory by taking up arms—but for the less scholastically inclined, it was one way to emoluments and power. Military commissions could often be purchased for cash.

The New Warlords

Quite a few of the twentieth-century warlords came from the new-style military colleges with foreign instructors. Some, like Wu Peifu, one of the most powerful and durable warlords of central China, were scholars in their own right. One of the most famous, Feng Yuxiang, was a devout Christian; another was a utopian socialist. But all were profoundly affected by their knowledge of the historical wars and martial arts of China. They fought as though playing a chess game; indeed chess was considered in China an excellent metaphor for warfare.

Colourful and swaggering though many of the warlords were, some of them were thoughtful men who understood the crisis that had overtaken China. But their own inability to unite in the cause of patriotism brought all such ideas to naught.

They killed without compunction—their own men, if they breached discipline; the enemy's troops; often civilians, if they resisted rape or plunder. They used horrible tortures—death by minute slicing of the flesh; suspension by the neck in bamboo or wooden cages; breaking the victim's knees on a pile of chains; slicing limbs off bit-by-bit in a haychopping guillotine; branding on the face, and so on. Beating the thighs with bamboo poles until they were bruised and lacerated, and the bones fractured, was considered mild. The best any victim could hope for was the quick beheading at which Chinese executioners were expert. The heads were displayed on spikes, or over city walls and gates for the edification of the general public. Man's inhumanity to man was brought by the Chinese to a fine art.

It should be recalled that all this was not exclusive to China. The foreigners who laudably denounced torture came from societies where such things had been commonplace only two or three centuries before. And the refinements of the use of electricity, gas chambers, and horrifying medical experiments with live patients, were still things of the future in Europe. . . .

A Spiral of Fragmentation

After the death of Yuan Shikai, the centralized control of the armed forces of the Republic—already shaky since the 1911 Revolution—ceased to exist. Until the Northern Expedition in 1926 the authority of the Kuomintang [Nationalist Party] barely extended beyond Guangdong province, leaving a central power vacuum. The country was plunged into a spiral of greater and greater fragmentation, in which the actual divisions within China were unclear and constantly shifting. As a convenient shorthand, commentators at the time often talked of China as divided into two amorphous groupings—the 'Northerners', based in Peking, and the 'Southerners', based in Canton. Northerners were seen as traditional, unprincipled, and venal, a procession of warlords who succeeded one another in Peking with apparent casualness. Southerners were different. They were revolutionaries, who wanted to change China and restore it to its rightful position in the world. They had a conspicuous, long-term leader, Sun Yat-sen, an ideology of nationalism and (it was widely feared) socialism, and a party, the Kuomintang. Their major ambition was to launch a northern expedition which would reunify China and get rid of the northern warlords and the foreign imperialists.

The reality was less simple. Much of China was controlled neither by the Northerners or the Southerners, but by regional warlords. The Northerners' chief common characteristics were that they lived in the north, and that they were continuously involved in clique fighting with each other—among the Anfu, Zhili, and Fengtian cliques. The Southerners were more united, but much weaker; they had great difficulty in establishing and maintaining even a tiny base in Canton, and though Sun Yatsen tried twice to launch his Northern Expedition, he failed both times.

Sun died in 1925, one year before the actual Northern Expedition was launched. By this time the base in Canton and surrounding Guangdong province had been consolidated, in part with the help of Soviet advisers, sent to Canton as a result of an agreement between Sun Yatsen and Moscow in 1923. One of the leading figures in the emergence of the southern military was Chiang Kaishek, who himself had been to Moscow for military training. On his return in 1924 he started the training of the revolutionary army which would sweep through China in 1926 and 1927 on the Northern Expedition. Chiang was the overall commander for the expedition, but much of the front-line fighting was done by Guangdong armies not directly under his control, notably the Fourth (Iron) Army, or armies which had only recently joined the Kuomintang, such as the Seventh Army from Guangxi.

With the breakdown of even a pretence of centralized command, officers commanding forces from company or even platoon size upwards became a law unto themselves in the areas they occupied. Thus, although history mainly remembers a score or so of famous big warlords, with whole armies under their command, China was actually administered—if one could call it that—by thousands of middle-rank officers whose loyalty to their superiors at, say, the provincial level was tenuous to say the least.

The other well-trodden path to warlord status was banditry. Destitute peasants, small artisans, or unemployed soldiers roamed the countryside, living off what little plunder they could find. Since the warlord armies were often paid and fed through levies and confiscations from the civilian population, the latter had little to choose between anarchy caused by bandits or 'government' by whichever warlord was dominant in their locality. Some soldiers hovered perpetually between banditry and the service of warlords. From the warlords they usually got only small and irregular pay, but at least clothing and food were guaranteed and there was a chance in the course of military campaigns of looting in towns and cities, where the pickings were better than in the countryside. Merchants either hired armed guards to protect their goods in transit, or took the chance of paying *lijin* (tolls) to warlord troops or being robbed and perhaps murdered by bandits. Banditry was no great social stigma for those who later rose to prominence in more-or-less respectable commands. . . .

The inherent contradictions between a life centred on war, and the doctrines of important religions or progressive political creeds, make it understandable that the great majority of the warlords—with a few outstanding exceptions—were dedicated to just three things: their personal security, pleasure, and self-aggrandisement. In warfare they changed sides according to the progress of a campaign, and if the commander did not care to go over to the enemy when the going got sticky, his men might make the decision for him by defecting.

The New Culture Movement and the May Fourth Movement

BY R. KEITH SCHOPPA

Despite China's political instability during the warlord period (1916–1927), when the country was ruled by regional strongmen, the era was so vibrant with intellectual exploration that it is referred to as the Chinese Renaissance. China's universities saw the emergence of the New Culture Movement, an intellectual movement that favored the adoption of common, not classical, Chinese language, the rejection of traditional Confucian values, and experimentation with new ideas. Unlike the Self-Strengthening Movement of the late nineteenth century, or the Qing emperor's attempt at political reform in 1898, intellectuals in the New Culture Movement were not afraid to consider the complete reformation of Chinese society.

Growing nationalism associated with this intellectual movement led to a major political movement—the May Fourth Movement. Japan had seized the Chinese province of Shandong from occupying German troops during World War I. At the war's end, world leaders at the Versailles Conference decided to grant Japan possession of Shandong. On May 4, 1919, students and workers took to Beijing's streets and Tiananmen Square in patriotic protest. Their demonstration in Beijing was the first protest in a movement that soon spread across China.

R. Keith Schoppa, Doehler Professor of Asian History at Loyola College in Maryland, describes both the New Culture Movement and the May Fourth Movement in this excerpt from his book The Columbia Guide to Modern Chinese History. *He is also the author of* Chinese Elites and Political Change: Zhejiang Province in the Early Twentieth Century.

R. Keith Schoppa, *The Columbia Guide to Modern Chinese History*. New York: Columbia University Press, 2000. Copyright © 2000 by Columbia University Press. Reproduced with permission.

While Confucianism as an ideology had officially ended with the abolition of the civil service examination in 1905, it retained its stranglehold on the social and ethical aspects of Chinese society. In family life, the ancient Confucian social bonds emphasizing the importance of age and the male gender retained their sway, elevating the status and power of parents over children, of men over women. Children were betrothed by matchmakers in marriages to benefit families, not individuals. If one's fiancé died before marriage or if one's husband died early, the unmarried or widowed woman must remain forever chaste, choosing death rather than becoming once again intimately involved. Young women were forbidden by mothers-in-law to unbind their feet or to attend school. The power of "Confucius and sons" was literally that of life and death.

With the collapse of old verities and institutions and with the rise of new social and political alternatives, there should be little surprise that slogans like "Down with Confucius and sons" began to fill new newspapers and journals and to echo in street demonstrations. Sometimes the language of the slogan was acted out in the taking of life itself. A young woman in the distant interior of Gansu threw herself down a well rather than deal with a mother-in-law who forbade her to unbind her feet. In Hunan, a Miss Zhao, betrothed to a man she despised, slit her throat as she was being carried in her bridal chair. Sons disregarded parental wishes and even orders regarding life decisions. Suicide rates tell the tragic story: among Chinese women, suicide rates were highest among those in their late teens and twenties; in the early twentieth century, such suicides occurred at a rate more than double that of Japan, and ten times that of Sweden.

The New Culture Movement

One extraordinarily influential vehicle for the expression of contempt for the old and hope for a new social and cultural world was the journal *New Youth,* whose publication began in 1915. Edited by a returned student from France, Chen Duxiu, the journal called on the young to struggle "to exert [their] intellect, discard resolutely the old and the rotten, regard them as enemies," and to be independent, progressive, dynamic, cosmopolitan, and scientific. With a circulation of up to sixteen thousand copies, the journal was read by students in all parts of China. Not only did it offer a forum for students to discuss issues, but from 1917 on it was written in the vernacular.

To that point, the language of printed materials, whether books, newspapers, or journals, had been classical or literary Chinese. The syntax of the classical style was difficult: it valued concision, often omitting subjects and objects; it was marked by characters that served as particles giving the sentence a tone or a particular turn; and it used no punctuation. Traditional scholars had apparently believed that anyone intelligent enough to read the classical language should be intelligent enough to know where to punctuate it. But because of the concision, the particles, and the lack of punctuation, it was not only difficult but open to all sorts of ambiguity. In addition, it had two other strikes against it: it was a great obstacle to increased literacy among the Chinese masses, and the development of a modern Chinese nation-state required a more literate public—reform of language thus was crucial. . . .

Another strong proponent of the vernacular, or *baihua*, was Hu Shi, who had completed his doctorate at Columbia University, studying with philosopher John Dewey. Chen and Hu became colleagues at Beijing University, which, like Chen's *New Youth*, emerged as central in what came to be known as the New Culture Movement. Established in the Manchu reform effort of the early twentieth century, Beijing University did not have a reputation as a serious institution of study or research; rather, an education there was seen as a ticket to a governmental bureaucratic position. Appointed university chancellor in 1916, Cai Yuanpei was determined to change the reputation and the reality. If a new language was to form the basis for a new culture that was to be forged by the young, then Beijing University should be the laboratory where the shaping of that culture should be centered. Cai thus gathered scholars of every intellectual and political stripe at the university to discuss possibilities for the new China, to debate ideas about the form and shape of China's modern state, and to argue and contend in an atmosphere of unfettered academic freedom. The excitement among faculty and students involved in trying to devise a blueprint for modern China must have been almost palpable.

An Intellectual Revolution

Although the phrase came to be associated with a policy of Mao Zedong in the 1950s, the New Culture Movement, extending into the mid-1920s, was a period when "a hundred schools of thought" contended. In essence, the movement was an intellectual revolution. . . .

The milieu of intellectual quest was stimulated during these years by lecture tours of foreigners of various intellectual persuasions. Hu Shi's teacher John Dewey spent 1919 and 1920 living and lecturing in China, spreading his message of pragmatism.

CONFUCIANISM REJECTED

Chen Duxiu (1879–1942) was a French-educated Chinese intellectual and leader of the New Culture Movement. His thinking led him to reject Confucianism in the pages of his magazine New Youth. *In this excerpt from an article first published in December 1916, Chen clearly rejects Confucianism as being associated with the old feudal China that he wanted to change.*

Confucius lived in a feudal age. The ethics he promoted is the ethics of the feudal age. The social mores he taught and even his own mode of living were teachings and modes of a feudal age. The objectives, ethics, social norms, mode of living, and political institutions did not go beyond the privilege and prestige of a few rulers and aristocrats and had nothing to do with the happiness of the great masses. How can this be shown? In the teachings of Confucius, the most important element in social ethics and social life is the rules of decorum and the most serious thing in government is punishment. In chapter one of the *Book of Rites,* it is said that "The rules of decorum do not go down to the common people and the penal statutes do not go up to the great officers." [1:35] Is this not solid proof of the [true] spirit of the way of Confucius and the spirit of the feudal age?

Ch'en Tu-hsiu, "The Way of Confucianism and Modern Life," in *Changing China: Readings in the History of China from the Opium War to the Present.* New York: Praeger, 1977, pp. 172–75.

In 1921 and 1922, philosopher Bertrand Russell lectured widely not only on his intellectual interest of mathematical logic but also on pacifism, a subject that in the violent warlord period must have struck many chords. Margaret Sanger, feminist and birth-control advocate, lectured in China in 1922, her ideas harmonizing with the period's emphasis on women's liberation. The visit of Nobel laureate Rabindranath Tagore, of India, in 1924 touched off a heated debate over Tagore's message extolling Asian cultures and warning about the importation of too much Western civilization. Such foreign lectures served as validation for some of the new ideas emerging in the intellectual debates, even as they prodded and stimulated more thought and involved more and more people in the debates.

Tagore and his supporters aside, there were widespread calls for two "men" whose backgrounds were clearly in the West and whose names became watchwords at the time and for much of the twentieth century: Mr. De and Mr. Sai. Mr. De(mocracy) became the rallying cry of those who bemoaned the shambles of the Chinese state, destroyed and undercut by warlords and venal politicians and bureaucrats. Though the memory of the brief burst of democracy in 1912 and 1913 was fading, the promise of democracy seemed strengthened by the victory of the "democratic" Allied powers in World War I and by the Bolshevik revolution in Russia. Mr. Sai (Mr. Science) was in the vanguard of the modern world; whatever was "scientific" seemed progressive. Science was seen as an instrument of enlightenment. To follow the scientific path seemed to promise the best for the future of the nation and the individual. Though a few intellectuals bemoaned the use to which science had been put by the West, seeing in the destructiveness of the war the bankruptcy of Western values, the vast majority of Chinese saw science as a panacea for the country's ills.

The May Fourth Movement

The New Culture Movement is part of what is generally known as the May Fourth Movement, an amorphous range of activities that can be dated from the founding of *New Youth* in 1915 to 1923 or 1924 and that, taken together, can be considered a cultural revolution. The movement takes its name from a demonstration, primarily of students, in Beijing on May 4, 1919, a nationalistically charged incident that substantially changed the direction and import of the whole cultural revolution effort. After Japan had seized German-held Shandong, the island-nation spent the war years concluding secret agreements with Allied powers confirming its right to maintain control of the province. Not surprisingly then, world leaders at the postwar Versailles Conference decided to allow Japan to continue to hold Shandong Province. In reaction, on May 4 about three thousand students from thirteen area colleges marched from Tian'anmen Square to the foreign-legation quarters to protest this decision. Marked by sporadic violence and numbers of arrests, the demonstration was the first salvo in what became a nationwide protest movement.

In the capital, the demonstration led to the establishment of a citywide student union, bringing together students from middle schools and high schools with those from colleges and universities; women students were specifically included. This student union served as prototype for similar organizations in Shanghai, Wuhan, Tianjin, and other cities, and ultimately for a Student Union of the Republic of China, established in June. Students served as the yeast, as it were, in a rising nationalistic ferment. At Shanghai especially, patriotic sentiment spread among businessmen, merchants, and laborers, culminating in a general strike beginning on June 5. Its goal: to try to force the Chinese delegation at Versailles to refuse to sign the peace treaty. Its trump card was that Shanghai was the economic heart of the Republic of China and that a long general strike could bring an already weak economy to its knees. The extent of the rising tide of nationalism can be seen in that even notorious underworld organizations, the Green and Red gangs, ordered their members not to disrupt the strike. The announcement on July 2 that the delegation at Versailles had refused to sign the treaty meant that the efforts of the student unions and the general strike among a wide array of the populace had led to a political victory.

The Movement Splits

Such a positive result from the perspective of patriotic Chinese had crucial ramifications for the direction of the May Fourth Movement. Two main camps began to emerge in what would become a struggle for the heart of the movement. There were those who began to point to the spring and summer of 1919 as what could be accomplished through direct political action: politically inspired organizations and a general strike had forced the government to act as the students and strikers had wanted. In order to change China, why not continue this kind of political action? How, they argued, can we build a modern Chinese culture while people who hold political power retain the power to jail and even shoot down those who are in the vanguard of modern change? First, they asserted, we must change the political system to one more conducive to other modern changes. Direct, even violent, political action must become the central focus of activity. A leading proponent of this view was Chen Duxiu, the *New Youth* editor and dean of the School of Letters at Beijing University.

The other camp contended that any meaningful political change must be preceded by, and therefore must be built upon, cultural change. By the nature of things, according to proponents of this view, cultural change cannot be engineered rapidly by tools like violence; it is a slow effort based more on evolutionary rather than revolutionary dynamics. One of the most important advocates of this path was Hu Shi, whose own predilections and education under Dewey must surely have inspired this solution. Academic study and reform were the keys. "There is no liberation *in toto* or reconstruction *in toto*. Liberation means liberation from this or that institution, from this or that belief, for this or that individual; it is liberation bit by bit, drop by drop." For this reason, Hu attacked what he called *isms,* overarching systemic blueprints that offered a way out of China's predicament; specific problems, he argued, called for specific solutions, not for all-embracing creeds or systems. . . .

The *isms* that received increasing attention for their possibilities in dealing with China's problems were Marxism, and after the success of the Bolsheviks in 1917, Leninism. A year after the Russian Revolution, *New Youth* commemorated the anniversary, and six months later (May 1919) the journal devoted a complete issue to articles on Marxism. Intellectuals and journalists formed small study groups in Shanghai and Beijing to discuss socialism and Marxism. Mao Zedong, a student at Beijing University, returned to his home in Hunan Province to form such a study group. The Shanghai Marxist Study Society was the first cell in what would become the Chinese Communist Party. Agents from the Communist International (Comintern) made their first linkage to Shanghai and Beijing intellectuals, who were more and more committed to Marxism in 1920. The party was formally organized in July 1921. . . .

A Milestone

Historians have generally ranked the May Fourth Movement alongside the abolition of the civil service examination and the toppling of the monarchy and imperial regime as one of the most significant revolutionary milestones in the course of China's twentieth-century revolution. The first two milestones cast off the old and necessitated the as-yet-unknown new; this third milestone, while also casting off the old, began for the first time an earnest search for the new. Certainly it is an important demarcation in the intellectual and cultural history of China. It has been called China's Renaissance, perhaps in part because of the beginning use of the vernacular; it was in the Renaissance that writing in the Western vernaculars first came into practice. It has also been called the Chinese Enlightenment, a term recalling the important role of science and experimentation and the casting out of tradition. It may be called a cultural revolution, bringing to mind the Cultural Revolution of the 1960s and 1970s, in which the old and traditional were discarded, even trashed.

Because of its discarding of traditional Chinese culture, it has drawn strong reactions from various political forces whose self-definition has had almost necessarily to take a stand on the meaning of the traditional culture for a modern Chinese nation-state. For the Nationalist regime of Chiang Kai-shek and his successors, it seemed too radical a movement, destroying much good that lay in Chinese tradition and linked too closely with the rise of Chinese Communism. The Nationalists viewed the movement with considerable distrust and suspicion. The Communists, whose party grew out of the intellectual ferment and issues of the movement, while looking kindly on the May Fourth period have looked askance at the first phase, which emphasized the role of intellectuals in enlightening society so as to realize individual aspirations. Condemning emphasis on the individual as "bourgeois," the Communists throughout their history have struck out at both those who maintained such a mentality and intellectuals in general, holding that the group, by nature, seemed tainted with the toxin of individualism. Thus, the reaction of both major political parties has been tinged with negativism about this crucial modern movement.

Chiang Kai-shek and the Struggle Between the Nationalists and Communists

By Justus D. Doenecke

When Sun Yat-sen died in 1925, Chiang Kai-shek took his place as leader of the Guomindang (Kuomintang or Nationalist Party). Nationalists and the Communist Party joined together in the first United Front to defeat the warlords and to unify China. Chiang then turned on his Communist allies in 1927 and initiated a bloody purge. A long civil war ensued. Eventually, in order to survive, the Communists escaped to the countryside in an epic retreat remembered as the Long March (1934). Chiang ruled the Nationalist government from his capitol in Nanjing from 1928 to 1937.

In 1931, Japan seized the northern region of China known as Manchuria and established a puppet government and nation known as Manchukuo. The Japanese initiated an all-out military invasion of China six years later (1937). Now Chiang fought the Japanese as well as the Communists. For a brief time, the Communists and Chiang's Guomindang worked together in a second United Front to struggle against Japanese aggression, but when Japan was defeated in World War II, full-scale civil war broke out between the Guomindang and the Communists.

The Communists emerged as the victors in 1949. Chiang fled to Taiwan, where he claimed until his death in 1975 that his regime was the true government of China. In the following selection, Justus D. Doenecke, professor of history in New College of the University of South Florida in Sarasota, traces Chiang's turbulent career.

Justus D. Doenecke, *Historic World Leaders*. Farmington Hills, MI: Gale Research, 1994. Copyright © 1994 by The Gale Group, Inc. Reproduced by permission.

Chiang Kai-Shek was born Chiang Jui-yuan (meaning "Auspicious Beginning") in the tiny village of Chikow, near the foreign treaty port of Ningbo (Ningpo), on October 30, 1887. (Years later, a teacher gave him a courtesy name that meant "Boundary Stone" and was pronounced "Kai-shek" in Cantonese)....

Deciding to become a soldier in 1905, he cut his pigtail as an act of rebellion and went to Tokyo, the recognized center of military studies in Asia. While in Japan, Chiang was initiated into a revolutionary party, the *Tung Meng Hui* (Society of the Common Cause), and met China's leading nationalist leader Dr. Sun Yat-sen and his gifted disciple Chen Chi-mei. A typical revolutionary, young Chiang Kai-Shek was ardently nationalistic, indeed xenophobic, hating the "foreign" line of Manchu emperors and seeking to end China's degradation. Aware of Chiang's revolutionary sympathies, the Japanese imperial military academies refused to admit him, but his trip had not been wasted....

Revolutions Bring Chiang to Sun's Rescue

In October 1911, the so-called "Wunchang Uprising" took place, ending the 250-year-old rule of the Manchu-Qing (Ch'ing) Dynasty. When Chen Chi-mei became military governor of Shanghai that November, Chiang returned home as one of Chen's regimental commanders, beginning his rise in the military hierarchy of the embryonic Chinese republican movement, then engaged in a bitter struggle against China's new dictator Yüan Shikai. On May 18, 1916, Yüan had Chen Chi-mei assassinated, and on June 6, Yüan himself died.

China was plunged into a decade of chaos, marked by political anarchy and foreign intervention. Though the country had a common currency, postage, and diplomatic corps, it was a legal fiction. Rival regimes were located in Guangzhou (Canton) and Beijing (Peking), both claiming to be the legitimate Chinese government. Real power, however, was located in regional military governors, or warlords, some 200 or so bemedaled generals who pillaged the nation. Chiang at various times was reported as being a guerilla leader, brokerage clerk, and speculator on the Shanghai stock exchange. In the fall of 1917, Chiang moved to Guangzhou, where he served as an officer of the local warlord, Chen Chiungming, commander of the Guangdong (Kwantung) army. At first, Chen Chiungming served as the protector of Dr. Sun, who in September 1917 declared himself "generalissimo" of a National Military government and who in April 1921 had been named "president" of a Chinese People's Government by a rump parliament. Formally, Chiang was Sun's personal military adviser and chief of the field operations department of the Guangdong (Kwantung) army. In reality, he was Sun's security chief and liaison.

Yet by early 1922, Sun had broken with Chen, fearing that the warlord was becoming too powerful; Chen in turn disapproved of Sun's plans for using Guangzhou as the base of a national unification drive. On June 16, when Chen attacked Sun's presidential headquarters, hoping to kill the Chinese leader, Chiang Kai-Shek helped the desperate Sun take refuge on a gunboat. As food was scarce and the water supply low, both men lived for 56 days in spartan surroundings. At night, Chiang would sneak ashore in search of food. In the daytime, he would scrub the decks. The two men became close, with Chiang—who was utterly devoted to Sun—assuming duties as Sun's chief of staff in October. In January of 1923, Sun was back in Guangzhou.

Sun's New Party Aligns with Communists

By now, Sun had turned for support to the revolutionary regime in Moscow, and in September 1923, Chiang headed a delegation to study the Soviet military and social system. For the next two months, he visited various ministries and inspected the Kronstadt naval base near Petrograd. He left Russia with a negative impression, finding the country on the verge of a major power struggle between Leon Trotsky and Joseph Stalin and possessing imperialist aspirations in Outer Mongolia. Sun, however, welcomed Soviet assistance, particularly as he was receiving no encouragement from the Western powers. He even reorganized his Party, the *Kuomintang* (KMT), on Leninist lines, with all authority coming from the top down.

When, in January 1924, the KMT held its first party congress, Chiang was appointed to the Military Council. In May, Chiang became commandant of the new KMT Military Academy at Whampoa, ten miles down river from Guangzhou. Realizing that he needed a well-trained army to overcome the warlords, Sun saw Whampoa as the indispensable instrument of national unification. Though Chiang developed a core cadre of officers that would be personally loyal to him throughout his life, he could not yet crack the alliance Sun had made with the Soviet Union and the fledgling Chinese Communist Party. Indeed Zhou Enlai (Chou En-lai) was director of Whampoa's political department.

What was later called the Whampoa Clique soon made its mark. The Guangzhou business community had seen Sun depriving it of customs duties, threatening increased taxes, and welcoming Communists to its movement. There were many rumors that a pro-business coup was in the midst. On October 14, 1924, in what was called Bloody Wednesday, Chiang's Whampoa cadets, aided by Communist workers, routed the Merchant Volunteer Corps of Guangzhou. Whole sections of the city were burned. In March 1925, Chiang captured Shantou, the main base of Chen Chiungming.

When Sun died on March 12, Chiang briefly shared China's leadership with Wang Ching-wei and Hu Hanmin, leaders respectively of the KMT left and right wings. But in the "March 20th incident" of 1926, he seized the *Chungsha*n (the same gunboat to which he and Sun had fled in 1922), jailed such Communists as Zhou Enlai, and forced Wang Ching-wei to retire. Leading Communists, like the acting head of the propaganda department, Mao Zedong, were purged. By these sudden and swift moves, Chiang had gained control of Sun's total movement, an event confirmed on May 15, when he became the KMT's chairman.

Yet Chiang did not break with the Communists completely, for he needed them for his march north. In July of 1926, acting as supreme commander of the Northern Expeditionary Forces, he started an expedition in which six main armies defeated or absorbed 34 forces of the warlords. During the march, journalists bestowed upon him Sun's title of generalissimo, or "the gissimo" for short. (His wife became "the missimo.")

On March 22, 1927, Chiang occupied Shanghai, which had already been softened by a general strike of 80,000 workers led by Zhou Enlai. Two days later, Chiang seized Nanjing (Nanking), which he proclaimed as China's new capital. His troops struck northward through Hunan and Hubei (Hupei), then moved eastward through Jiangxi (Kiangsi) and Fujian (Fukien) toward the rich provinces of the lower Yangtze. Chiang had taken less than a year to bring the wealthy and populous provinces of southern, central, and eastern China under Nationalist control.

National Government Proclaimed in Nanjing

In the words of China expert John K. Fairbank, when Chiang captured Shanghai he "suddenly ceased to be a revolutionary." At 4:00 a.m. on April 12, 1927, Chiang called on his "Green Gang" allies, composed of a 1,000 armed civilians, to attack the city's major trade unions. In the days of terror that followed, thousands were killed. His "party purification" movement, aimed particularly at the Communists, soon spread through other provinces. The break between Chiang and the Communists was now final, and despite uneasy truces it was never to be healed.

Within a week, Chiang proclaimed a national government in Nanjing, and two months later, in alliance with warlord Feng Yuxiang, he precipitated the collapse of the KMT leadership centered at Wuhan. Much to the astonishment of Shanghai's bankers and industrialists, he launched what China specialist Jonathan D. Spence calls "a reign of terror" against the city's wealthiest inhabitants, thereby raising the millions of dollars he needed to pay his troops and continue the Northern Expedition.

By August 1927, however, Chiang had resigned his posts, a familiar Chiang tactic in times of trouble. Lack of funds, the continuing hostility of the Wuhan leaders, and a defeat by warlord forces at the strategic rail junction at Xuzhou all played a part. . . .

In line with the adage "never resign until you are indispensable," on January 9, 1928, Chiang reassumed his post of army commander-in-chief, launching the second stage of the Northern Expedition. In June, Beijing had fallen, and by the end of the year the KMT flag—a white sun on a blue and red ground—flew from Guangzhou to Mukden. That October, Chiang was made chairman of the State Council, the ruling body of 16 that constituted the top level of government. At age 41, he possessed overriding authority. Yet, anxious to get on with the "real business" of fighting Communists, Chiang did not dislodge such warlords as Yen Xi-shan and Feng Yuxiang, who never recognized his authority and would supply him with troops only when convenient.

Domestic Problems Abound

Chiang's problems were just beginning. His government was too small to provide adequate services to an impoverished population of 400 million. Illiteracy was widespread and transportation was primitive. Warlordism still remained, particularly above the Yangtze River. At times, even erstwhile supporters would break from Chiang to form regimes of their own. The ruling KMT itself was splintered into various factions. With entire warlord armies joining the Party and the admission of timeservers from the old bureaucracy, by 1932, even Chiang was disillusioned by the Party.

In every sphere of activity, Chiang found the tasks insuperable. True, urban life underwent radical transformation, and cities were soon marked by hospitals, secondary schools, universities, power stations, airports, and cinemas. Telegraph poles were planted; telephone wires radiated out to the remote regions; 75,000 miles of road were laid; and scholarship and archaeology flourished. Furthermore, until the late 1930s, the value of China's currency was quite stable, and in 1932 the budget was balanced. Only when the U.S. raised the price it would pay for silver did that metal—the basis of China's currency—leave China in great quantities. The average Chinese experienced more prosperity in the years 1929 to 1936 than at any time until the 1980s.

On the farm, however, crops were still harvested by hand, infant mortality was prevalent, and many girls were still forced to bind their feet. Scientific agriculture, railroads, a national press and communications system, and opportunities for youth and women were all desperately needed, and all such problems were enormously compounded by lack of funds.

Chiang entrusted ideological molding to the KMT Central Political Institute, who promulgated an anti-Communist, anti-imperialist nationalism interspersed with doses of the Confucian values of order, hierarchy, and discipline. By the early 1930s, Chiang had launched the Blueshirts, a carefully selected group of several thousand army officers. Its slogan was "Nationalize, Militarize, Productivize." Serving as a disciplined military and secret-police apparatus and swearing personal loyalty to Chiang, it engaged in political intimidation, perhaps even assassination of Chiang opponents.

Early in 1934, Chiang launched a "New Life Movement," an amorphous ideology that, in his words, would create "a new national consciousness and mass psychology" that would lead in turn to "the social regeneration of China." It combined the doctrines of Dr. Sun and missionary teachings with four Confucian principles translated loosely as "prosperity, justice, honesty, and a sense of self-respect." It fostered modesty in women's dress, abhorred casual sex, and frowned on public spitting, urinating, smoking in public, and wiping one's nose on a sleeve. Once the lessons of the movement were absorbed, Chiang said that China would be ready to solve "the four great needs": clothing, housing, food, and transportation.

To China's domestic woes were added equally difficult foreign problems. In September 1931, Japan invaded Manchuria, and Chiang felt forced to withdraw his forces south of the Great Wall. Facing a crisis among his supporters because of his arrest of Hu Hanmin, a KMT leader sympathetic to the Soviet Union, he could not afford a large-scale conflict. From a military standpoint, Chiang's judgment was sound, but in the eyes of his countrymen he appeared unwilling to stand up to foreign invasion.

Chiang briefly resigned from office, returning in January of 1932. Concentrating more power in his person than ever, he made himself chief of the General Staff and chairman of the National Military Council. Relying upon such German advisers as General Hans von Seeckt, who had streamlined his nation's army in the 1920s, Chiang sought to modernize China's army. According to the constitution designed by Dr. Sun, China was to be governed by five *yuan* or bureaus (executive, legislative, control, judicial, and examination). However, the yuans neither checked his action nor prevented continued concentration of funds in Chiang's Military Affairs Commission, which in reality was the de facto government of China.

Return to Power to Face More Internal Conflict

Upon Chiang's return to power, he was more determined than ever to eliminate the Chinese Communist movement. The Japanese, he would say, were "a disease of the skin," the Communists "a disease of the heart." He was made commander-in-chief of a Bandit Suppression Headquarters, which had dictatorial powers in regions where Communists were active. In 1934, as a result of a major assault, he destroyed two-thirds of the Communist forces. On October 16, 1934, 100,000 Communists, led by Mao Zedong, began their famous Long March, the arduous and circuitous retreat 5,000 miles to the distant northwest. While Chiang based his support on the urban business class, younger members of the rural élite and the less impoverished gentry, Mao attracted the poorer peasants and alienated intellectuals.

On December 12, 1936, Chiang was kidnapped at Xi'an (Sian) by Manchurian warlord Zhang Xueliang. Chiang had appointed the "Young Marshal," as he was called, to fight Communists. Upon learning that the Young Marshal was fraternizing with Mao's units in the hopes of cementing an anti-Japanese coalition, Chiang flew to Xi'an to investigate. Units of Young Marshal's army stormed the generalissimo's headquarters in the hills outside the city. Most of Chiang's bodyguard were killed. Scaling the back wall of his compound in night clothes, Chiang hid in a mountain cave, but he was soon captured. Two weeks of negotiation followed, to which Communist leader Zhou Enlai was a part. Chiang agreed not only to suspend all attacks against the Communists but also to engage in major resistance against further Japanese inroads. The heat was now off the Communist forces, established in Yan'an (Yenan). When the released Chiang returned to Nanjing, he was greeted by a crowd of 400,000. He never forgave his captor, whom he kept under perpetual house arrest.

On July 7, 1937, as a result of a confusing incident at Marco Polo Bridge just outside of Beijing, full-scale war between China and Japan broke out. Whatever chance Chiang had of establishing a strong centralized Chinese state was lost forever. As Beijing and Tianjin (Tientsin) fell respectively on July 28 and 29, Chiang decided that Northern China must be expendable. He would concentrate his forces along the Yangtze.

On August 14, in a major strategic gamble, Chiang decided to deflect the Japanese from North China by a counter-thrust on their forces in Shanghai. His air forces bombed Japanese ships anchored off the city's docks. The Japanese, however, had been forewarned, and the Chinese bombers were inaccurate. Yet, for three months, Chiang's ill-equipped forces conducted an extraordinary heroic defense of the city and of the Yangtze River valley as well. The Japanese suffered 40,000 casualties but 60 percent of Chiang's finest forces, some 250,000 troops, were killed or wounded. Hence the generalissimo lacked the trained forces needed to defend Hankou (Hankow), hundreds of miles away. He also could not prevent the Japanese capture of Nanjing on December 13. Here began three weeks of plunder that marked, in Spence's words, "a period of terror and destruction that must rank among the worst in the history of modern warfare." Chiang's armies were more successful in his defense of Taiyaun, where the Japanese advance stopped north of the Yellow River for two and a half years.

With the fall of Guangzhou in October 1938, Chiang had lost all of eastern China, with its industrial centers and the most fertile farmland in the nation. A million Japanese were occupying eight provinces, including every harbor along the coastline. During the war, Chiang lost half a million soldiers and 100 million civilians. Forced back to Chongqing (Chungking), which became his wartime capital, he could only engage in one strategy: trading land for time. Though Chiang's military moves were both correct and successful, he left vast areas of China open to penetration by Communist forces whose guerilla tactics won them popular acclaim.

Yet there was no question who directed the Chinese state. In March 1938, the KMT congress had granted Chiang the title of director general of the Party, a position formerly held by Dr. Sun. Remaining chairman of China's Military Affairs Commission, he had statutory power to "direct the people of the entire nation." In 1943, he added the position of president to his titles, and during the war years he held no fewer than 82 posts. When the Nationalist government retreated to the interior, Chiang's base of support started to shift from urban merchants and bankers, who accepted modernization and moderate reform in the countryside, to conservative landlords, who adhered strongly to standards of an older China.

Resources and Lack of Military Expertise Plague Nationalist Party

As Japan had conquered the comparatively prosperous Yangtze River valley, Chiang lacked the resources needed to rebuild an army. Hence, much of China's wartime inflation was undoubtedly inevitable. Chiang could be held more directly culpable for the starvation of possibly five million people: his government confiscated the food of the poorer peasants, then bungled relief efforts by incompetence and corruption. Little wonder the war was soon renewed. From January 7–13, 1941, Nationalist troops ambushed the Communist New Fourth Army, killing about 3,000 troops and making the break with Mao's legions almost absolute.

Franklin D. Roosevelt attempted to bolster Chiang's forces in a number of ways: loans, credits, planes, and material. The American president permitted "civilian" U.S. pilots to serve under Major General Claire Chennault as "Flying Tigers" and appointed one of America's best corps commanders, Lieutenant General Joseph Stilwell, to serve as Chiang's chief of staff. Roosevelt never envisioned Chinese territory as a major theater of war, but he possessed genuine personal respect for Chiang. He also feared China's internal collapse and surrender to the Japanese, believed that China could tie down several million Japanese troops, and saw China aiding in launching air attacks that might bring about a cheap victory. Roosevelt invited Chiang and his far more sophisticated wife to the Cairo Conference, held from November 22–26, 1943. In the summer of 1944, when it appeared as if the Chinese army was on the verge of collapse, Roosevelt was able to have Chiang give Stilwell command of all China's armed forces, but Chiang delayed the appointment, then refused the president altogether.

In Chiang's political treatise, *China's Destiny* (1943), he rejected Western-style liberalism and democracy, held foreigners responsible for all China's ills, and called for the eventual transformation of all capital into state capital. To the degree that Chiang had an ideology, it remained Confucianism, which—in his eyes—emphasized "complete loyalty to the state and . . . filial piety towards the nation."

By V-J Day, China was on the verge of civil war. In August 1945, U.S. ambassador Patrick J. Hurley sponsored negotiations whereby Chiang and Mao would agree to establish a political democracy, a unified military force, and equal legal status for all parties. All Chinese would have "freedom of person, religion, publication, and assembly." Moreover, Roosevelt's successor, Harry S. Truman, sent General George C. Marshall on a mediation mission. Any temporary truces, however, broke down quickly.

Militarily, Chiang managed the KMT effort badly. Rather than wage war from the wealthy Yangtze valley, he attempted to defend all of China. No strategist, Chiang attempted to retain all Manchuria, thereby stretching his forces too thinly and losing city after city, province after province. The Communists continually broke the rail links between Manchuria and China proper, and the Nationalist air force was not strong enough to make up the lost supplies. When he committed American-trained troops to the Northeast, he failed to consolidate control of the North China territory in between. In 1947, when he could have gained time by evacuating major cities, he refused.

Assuming direct command, rather than permitting local commanders to make on-the-spot decisions, his personal orders were both contradictory and impractical, causing his troops to desert in droves. Particularly damaging was the battle of Huai-hai on the central China plain, in which over one-third of a million KMT troops were taken prisoner.

On the civilian front Chiang did no better. His government mismanaged the economy, showing itself unable to control the rampant inflation, taxation, profiteering, and starvation. Such economic irresponsibility alienated the urban middle class while his obvious opposition to ending the civil war antagonized the already restless students. July of 1948 saw the senseless killing in Beijing of 14 unarmed students by government forces.

Chiang Returns to Taiwan

Postwar China attempted the forms of democracy without the substance. Late in 1946, the KMT convened a national assembly and drafted a constitution, but genuine democratic participation remained lacking. On April 19, 1948, the 3,000 member national assembly chose Chiang as president; Guangxi (Kwangsi) general Li Zongren (Li Tsungjen), a reformer, won the vice presidency over candidates more to Chiang's liking.

Such elections were soon made meaningless, for China was losing the civil war. On November 1, 1948, Mukden fell to the Communists, followed in two months by Beijing. On January 21, 1949, Chiang retired from the presidency, though he kept his post as head of the KMT. The hapless Li could not reverse the deteriorating situation, while Chiang's retirement partook more of fantasy than reality. The separation of roles was confusing, further hampering KMT resistance. Chiang viewed his departure as an opportunity to lay the onus of failure on someone else's shoulders. But whether in Fenghua or Shanghai, he continued to direct government operations and military campaigns.

Unable to build a bastion of resistance in southern or southwestern China, on December 10, 1949, Chiang retired to the island province of Taiwan, 100 miles off the coast of mainland China.

The Rape of Nanjing

By Iris Chang

One of the worst atrocities in the history of humankind occurred in Nanjing (Nanking), China, beginning in December 1937. For six weeks, Japanese troops occupied the city of Nanjing and then massacred hundreds of thousands of defenseless Chinese citizens. Scholars estimate that from 260,000 to 350,000 were killed in that short time period. Mass rapes of the city's female residents and the elimination of entire families were the norm.

Journalist Iris Chang describes some of the atrocities committed by the Japanese soldiers in this selection from her book The Rape of Nanking. *Chang writes that a "curtain of silence" fell over this event. She attributes that silence to Cold War politics. The United States wanted Japan's support to resist international communism, including Chinese communism, and the Japanese did not want revealed to the world what its troops had done in China. The Japanese have yet to fully admit or apologize for the atrocities. To this day there is considerable anti-Japanese sentiment in China because of what happened in China under Japanese occupation and especially because of Nanjing. Chang is also author of* Thread of the Silkworm *and recipient of the MacArthur Foundation's Program on Peace and International Cooperation award.*

Torture

The torture that the Japanese inflicted upon the native population at Nanking almost surpasses the limits of human comprehension. Here are only a few examples:

—*Live burials:* The Japanese directed burial operations with the precision and efficiency of an assembly line. Soldiers would force one group of Chinese captives to dig a grave, a second group to bury the first, and then a third group to bury the second and so on. Some victims were partially buried to their chests

Iris Chang, *The Rape of Nanking: The Forgotten Holocaust of World War II*. New York: BasicBooks, 1997. Copyright © 1997 by Iris Chang. Reproduced by permission.

or necks so that they would endure further agony, such as being hacked to pieces by swords or run over by horses and tanks.

—*Mutilation:* The Japanese not only disemboweled, decapitated, and dismembered victims but performed more excruciating varieties of torture. Throughout the city they nailed prisoners to wooden boards and ran over them with tanks, crucified them to trees and electrical posts, carved long strips of flesh from them, and used them for bayonet practice. At least one hundred men reportedly had their eyes gouged out and their noses and ears hacked off before being set on fire. Another group of two hundred Chinese soldiers and civilians were stripped naked, tied to columns and doors of a school, and then stabbed by *zhuizi*—special needles with handles on them—in hundreds of points along their bodies, including their mouths, throats, and eyes.

—*Death by fire:* The Japanese subjected large crowds of victims to mass incineration. In Hsiakwan a Japanese soldier bound Chinese captives together, ten at a time, and pushed them into a pit, where they were sprayed with gasoline and ignited. On Taiping Road, the Japanese ordered a large number of shop clerks to extinguish a fire, then bound them together with rope and threw them into the blaze. Japanese soldiers even devised games with fire. One method of entertainment was to drive mobs of Chinese to the top stories or roofs of buildings, tear down the stairs, and set the bottom floors on fire. Many such victims committed suicide by jumping out windows or off rooftops. Another form of amusement involved dousing victims with fuel, shooting them, and watching them explode into flame. In one infamous incident, Japanese soldiers forced hundreds of men, women, and children into a square, soaked them with gasoline, and then fired on them with machine guns.

—*Death by ice:* Thousands of victims were intentionally frozen to death during the Rape of Nanking. For instance, Japanese soldiers forced hundreds of Chinese prisoners to march to the edge of a frozen pond, where they were ordered to strip naked, break the ice, and plunge into the water to go "fishing." Their bodies hardened into floating targets that were immediately riddled with Japanese bullets. In another incident, the Japanese tied up a group of refugees, flung them into a shallow pond, and bombarded them with hand grenades, causing "an explosive shower of blood and flesh."

—*Death by dogs:* One diabolical means of torture was to bury victims to their waist and watch them get ripped apart by German shepherds. Witnesses saw Japanese soldiers strip a victim naked and direct German shepherds to bite the sensitive areas of his body. The dogs not only ripped open his belly but jerked out his intestines along the ground for a distance.

The incidents mentioned above are only a fraction of the methods that the Japanese used to torment their victims. The Japanese saturated victims in acid, impaled babies with bayonets, hung people by their tongues. One Japanese reporter who later investigated the Rape of Nanking learned that at least one Japanese soldier tore the heart and liver out of a Chinese victim to eat them. Even genitals, apparently, were consumed: a Chinese soldier who escaped from Japanese custody saw several dead people in the streets with their penises cut off. He was later told that the penises were sold to Japanese customers who believed that eating them would increase virility.

The Rapes

If the scale and nature of the executions in Nanking are difficult for us to comprehend, so are the scale and nature of the rapes. . . .

It is impossible to determine the exact number of women raped in Nanking. Estimates range from as low as twenty thousand to as high as eighty thousand. But what the Japanese did to the women of Nanking cannot be computed in a tally sheet of statistics. . . .

We do know, however, that it was very easy to be a rape victim in Nanking. The Japanese raped Nanking women from all classes: farm wives, students, teachers, white-collar and blue-collar workers, wives of YMCA employees, university professors, even Buddhist nuns, some of whom were gang-raped to death. And they were systematic in their recruitment of women. In Nanking Japanese soldiers searched for them constantly as they looted homes and dragged men off for execution. Some actually conducted door-to-door searches, demanding money and *hua gu niang*—young girls.

This posed a terrible dilemma for the city's young women, who were not sure whether to remain at home or to seek refuge in the International Safety Zone—the neutral territory guarded by Americans and Europeans. If they stayed in their houses, they ran the risk of being raped in front of their families. But if they left home in search of the Safety Zone, they ran the risk of being captured by the Japanese in the streets. Traps lay everywhere for the Nanking women. For instance, the Japanese army fabricated stories about markets where women could exchange bags of rice and flour for chickens and ducks. But when women arrived on the scene prepared to trade, they found platoons of soldiers waiting for them. Some soldiers employed Chinese traitors to seek out prospective candidates for rape. Even in the Safety Zone, the Japanese staged incidents to lure foreigners away from the refugee camps, leaving women vulnerable to kidnapping raids.

China Under Communism

Establishing a Communist State

By Debra E. Soled

The People's Republic of China was formally established in October 1949. Mao and his Communist government faced the daunting task of rebuilding a country devastated by years of war and social upheaval. Creating a new political system and rebuilding the economy were their first goals. The Communists restructured the government and created a National People's Congress. They also instituted land reform, formed agricultural collectives, restructured industry, and implemented five-year development plans. The Soviet Union provided both a model of a Communist state as well as much-needed technical assistance.

Editor Debra E. Soled presents an overview of this process in the following selection. Soled is coauthor of Christianity in China: A Scholar's Guide to Resources in the Libraries and Archives of the United States.

Great tasks lay before Mao Zedong (1893–1976) and the Communist leadership. To carry out their goal of transforming China's economy and society, Chinese leaders looked to the Soviet Union as a model, as well as a source of technology and aid. The Soviet experience offered structures for party and state organizations, models for urban-based and industrial development, and approaches toward collectivization of farming. At the same time, the Chinese Communist Party (CCP) leadership consciously limited its scope of activities during the initial years of transition, implementing policies gradually. The CCP also sought to avoid the mistakes and excesses of the Soviet experience. Although the Chinese Communist Party had long been dependent on Soviet support, it had sought to adapt Marxist-Leninist theories to Chinese realities from the very beginning. In particular, Mao's strategy based China's revolutionary struggle on the peasantry, rather than on the urban proletariat. And to help carry out his visions, Mao Zedong added a third theoretical source of ideas—Mao Zedong Thought.

The new government began by taking a united front approach, in which the proletariat was to join with the peasants, petty bourgeoisie, and national bourgeoisie to rule through a "people's democratic dictatorship." In addition to the Chinese Communist Party, non-CCP and non-Kuomintang (KMT) political parties sent delegates to the first Chinese People's Political Consultative Conference (CPPCC), an interim body that exercised the powers and functions of a national assembly until a system of people's congresses was established. The CPPCC approved a temporary constitution (the Common Program), elected Mao Zedong chairman of the People's Central Government Council and of the CPPCC National Committee, and determined administrative matters such as the national emblem and national flag. . . .

The CCP leaders consolidated power slowly, encountering pockets of resistance in places such as Tibet. China was temporarily divided into six military/administrative regions until formal government structures were established. In 1954, the Chinese People's Political Consultative Conference adopted a formal constitution, which outlined political and governing structures. The National People's Congress (NPC) was established as a permanent representative body. The NPC and its Standing Committee were elected by delegates, who were in turn elected by about 200,000 local assemblies. The NPC approved appointments to the State Council, and thus became the formal source of state authority; the CPPCC relinquished its legal power to become a deliberative and advisory body. However, the NPC's legislative authority was kept weak, and real power resided with the Chinese Communist Party.

Looking to the Soviet model, the Chinese Communist Party formed a government structure in which power was vested in three organizations: the party, the government bureaucracy, and the People's Liberation Army (PLA). The CCP Central Committee, consisting of 100 to 300 members, is elected by the delegates of the party congress. Actual power in the central government, however, is held by the Political Bureau (Politburo), particularly its Standing Committee.

One key to the CCP's victory in the civil war had been its successful mobilization of the peasants, who comprise 80 percent of China's population. The CCP helped peasants solve practical problems and improve their standards of living, both of which the Nationalists had neglected. In the 1930s, half the land was held by rich farmers in some regions, while the bulk of the rural population were tenants or landless peasants. Rent paid in the form of 40 to 60 percent of annual crops and land taxes kept the peasants at subsistence levels.

The reallocation of land through CCP land reform measures had started in North and Northeast China, where the CCP built its base after 1937. The goal now was to transform China into a socialist society and economy. The CCP leaders saw agricultural reform as the first step to nation-building. They also recognized the need to remove the rural elite and destroy the local power structure. . . .

To realize these goals, the rural population was divided into five classes: landlords, rich peasants, middle peasants, poor peasants, and agricultural laborers, with policies designed to benefit mainly the last two groups. A more equitable tax structure shifted the burden to the rich, rents were reduced, and land was redistributed.

The land ownership system was not abolished without resistance or bloodshed. At local levels, people's tribunals led struggles against the landlords. Much of the violence was carried out by vengeful peasants and local party cadres, although authorized by the CCP. Some 2 million landlords are estimated to have been killed during these years. By 1952, land confiscated from the landlords and rich peasants was redistributed under the administration of the *xiang,* a group of several villages.

Improving the livelihood of a majority of the people in the countryside did much to bolster the credibility of the new government. For many, the expression "after liberation" (*jiefang yihou*) held genuine meaning, contrasting favorably with the destitution and widespread undernourishment of previous decades. Nevertheless, many scholars feel that the main achievement of agricultural reform was political, while the direct impact on productivity was more modest. Using both coercive and persuasive methods, the CCP built the base on which further social transformation through collectivization of agriculture could be implemented. . . .

Collectivization of Rural Society

The CCP's vision of transforming China's society and economy started with the countryside. Party leaders had already had considerable success in mobilizing the peasants in North China, and by 1952, approximately 40 percent of households in the liberated areas had been organized into mutual aid teams. In this first stage, peasants pooled tools and draft animals and labored together, particularly during the planting and harvesting seasons. During a further experimental stage, households and villages were organized into larger units of production and administration, called Agricultural Producers' Cooperatives. Land was pooled in these semisocialist cooperatives, although individuals still held nominal deeds to the land.

The next several years saw cycles of intensive mobilization followed by relaxation of the collectivization process, as these ef-

MARRIAGE LAW OF 1950

The political system and economy were not the only aspects of Chinese society that the Communists worked to reform. Revolutionary changes also restructured family life. Here are some excerpts from the 1950 Marriage Law of the People's Republic of China that illustrate some of the changes.

ARTICLE 1. The feudal marriage system which is based on arbitrary and compulsory arrangement and the superiority of man over woman and ignores the children's interests shall be abolished.

The New-Democratic marriage system, which is based on the free choice of partners, on monogamy, on equal rights for both sexes, and on the protection of the lawful interests of women and children, shall be put into effect.

ARTICLE 2. Bigamy, concubinage, child betrothal, interference with the remarriage of widows, and the exaction of money or gifts in connection with marriages, shall be prohibited.

ARTICLE 3. Marriage shall be based upon the complete willingness of the two partners. Neither party shall use compulsion and no third party shall be allowed to interfere. . . .

ARTICLE 7. Husband and wife are companions living

forts met with support or resistance. In addition, food was sometimes in short supply, grain transfers to urban areas were inefficient, and government procurement prices kept rising. When problems became obvious, many party leaders urged slowing down the process. But Mao firmly believed that stepping up mobilization was the only way to achieve social transformation of the Chinese peasantry. He urged intensive drives to collectivize agriculture, beginning in 1955. The entire Chinese countryside (with the exception of national minority areas) was to be organized under higher level, or fully collectivized, Agricultural Producers' Cooperatives in which land, as well as tools, was to be jointly owned by the cooperative. . . .

together and shall enjoy equal status in the home.

ARTICLE 8. Husband and wife are in duty bound to love, respect, assist and look after each other, to live in harmony, to engage in productive work, to care for the children and to strive jointly for the welfare of the family and for the building up of the new society.

ARTICLE 9. Both husband and wife shall have the right to free choice of occupation and free participation in work or in social activities.

ARTICLE 10. Both husband and wife shall have equal rights in the possession and management of family property.

ARTICLE 11. Both husband and wife shall have the right to use his or her own family name.

ARTICLE 12. Both husband and wife shall have the right to inherit each other's property.

ARTICLE 13. Parents have the duty to rear and to educate their children; the children have the duty to support and assist their parents. Neither the parents nor the children shall maltreat or desert one another.

The foregoing provision also applies to foster-parents and foster-children. Infanticide by drowning and similar criminal acts are strictly prohibited.

J. Mason Gentzler, ed., *Changing China: Readings in the History of China from the Opium War to the Present.* New York: Praeger, 1977, pp. 268–72.

Industrial Priorities and the First Five-Year Plan

In the first Five-Year Plan period, CCP planners made an attempt to balance China's industrial base geographically. In contrast to the period before 1949, when factories in China had been concentrated in coastal cities, there was now a drive to build up new industrial centers in the northern, northwestern, and central parts of the country. Of the 156 planned projects in the first Five-Year Plan, nearly all were in heavy industry, such as iron and steel, electric power, and machinery. The Soviet Union transferred the latest technologies in the steel industry to plants to Baotou, Inner Mongolia; Wuhan, Hubei (Central China); and elsewhere. Other important large-scale plants included those producing automobiles in Changchun in the northeast and tractors in Luoyang, Henan. China also began to invest substantially in fuel exploration at this time, especially in the north and northwest provinces rich in coal, oil, natural gas, and other resources. The output of producer goods was impressive: production of machine tools doubled between 1952 and 1957; electric power generation increased tenfold.

A Critique of
Mao's Communist
Government

By Anonymous

*By 1957, it was becoming apparent that agricultural cooperatives orga-
nized by the government were proving to be a disappointment because
harvests had not significantly improved. Some government leaders began
to disband the cooperatives as they searched for more practical methods of
improving agricultural yields. Mao Zedong saw this as a threat to his revolutionary program. He wrote an essay in which he called upon those who
disagreed with his policies to speak out and offer suggestions. He said,
"Let a hundred flowers bloom and a hundred schools contend." Mao was
making a historical reference to the Zhou dynasty in which "one hundred
schools" of philosophy appeared, among them Confucianism and Taoism.*

*Thousands came forward with criticisms of Mao's policies, some of
which were quite detailed and intensely argued. Mao then decided that
some flowers were actually "poisonous weeds." He suppressed the Hundred Flowers, tracked down the critics when he could, and sent many to
the countryside for "reform through labor." To this day, scholars do not
know if Mao began with a sincere intent to seek constructive criticism or
if he was just trying to flush out his political opponents.*

*Here are selections from the text of one wall poster put up at
Qinghua University in 1957 that Mao would no doubt have considered
to be a "poisonous weed." The author passionately accuses Mao of living
an emperor's lifestyle while the people suffered and of using the People's
Liberation Army to oppress dissent. The author remains anonymous.*

I was born and raised in the liberated area. For twenty years
I've seen through the imperialists. Facing the enemy, my eyes
are red with anger and I would risk losing my head and

Anonymous, "I Accuse, I Protest," *Wild Lily, Prairie Fire: China's Road to Democracy,
Yun'an to Tian'anmen, 1942–1989*, edited by Gregor Benton and Alan Hunter.
Princeton, NJ: Princeton University Press, 1995. Copyright © 1995 by Princeton
University Press. Reproduced by permission.

shedding my blood; but facing the dictatorship of the Communist Party I am cowardly and powerless. How small and pitiful is one individual! We have given our blood, sweat, toil, and precious lives to defend not the people but the bureaucratic organs and bureaucrats who oppress the people and live off the fat of the land. They are a group of fascists who employ foul means, twist the truth, band together in evil adventure, and ignore the people's wish for peace both at home and abroad.

During the past few years the achievements in construction were used to deceive the people. What kind of construction? Both a luxurious superstructure divorced from the people and a national defense construction which is really an endless preparation for war. Various murderous acts against humanity are being carried out under cover of the word "peace" and given the beautified name of "Communist activities." Party, you are now betraying our nation and the innate goodness of our young people; you have smashed the peace. This is how I feel about you from the bottom of my heart.

What does it mean when the Communists say they suffer so that the people may not suffer and that they let the people enjoy things before they do the same? What do they mean when they speak of suffering now in order to have a happy life later? These are lies. We ask: Is Chairman Mao, who enjoys the best things of life and passes the summer at Jinwangdao and spends his vacations at Yuquanshan, having a hard time? Are the starving peasants, with only a cup of spring water, enjoying the good life? In Yan'an was Chairman Mao, who had two dishes plus soup for every meal, having a hard time? Were the peasants, who had nothing to eat but bitter vegetables, enjoying the good life? Everyone was told that Chairman Mao was leading a hard and simple life. That son of a bitch! A million shames on him! Scholars, try to find out the meaning of the words "good life" and "suffering." Never mind, you don't have any guts. Our pens can never defeat Mao Zedong's Party guards and his imperial army. When he wants to kill you, he doesn't have to do it himself. He can mobilize your wife and children to denounce you and then kill you with their own hands! Is this a rational society? This is class struggle, Mao Zedong style! This is the spiritual side of our age! . . .

The Chinese people have been deceived. When they courageously drove out the imperialists and the Chiang Kai-shek gang, they put their trust in the wrong man. We used a robber's knife to drive out another robber.

Let the Party send its special agents to arrest me! Let them expel me from the Party! But if I am killed, there are still thousands and tens of thousands of others who won't let the robber live in peace.

The Great Leap Forward Results in Famine

By Jasper Becker

Mao launched the Great Leap Forward in 1957. The goals of his economic program were to improve agricultural yields through collectivization and to increase industrial production. Millions of peasants were moved away from farming into small-scale industrial production. Those who continued to farm were organized into agricultural producers' cooperatives of forty to three hundred households. The results were disastrous. Harvests declined sharply and famine soon followed. Scholars estimate that more than 30 million people died of hunger in China between 1958 and 1961. Here British journalist Jasper Becker documents events in one region, the Xinyang prefecture of Henan Province, where local officials terrorized peasants into meeting agricultural production quotas, then lied to higher authorities by inflating statistics on harvest yields. Mao chose to believe the local officials' glowing reports of plentiful harvests rather than admit that people were starving. In Henan Province, the peasants were forced to eat grass, and eventually the dead bodies of their neighbors and relatives. Becker is Beijing Bureau Chief for the South China Morning Post *and author of* Hungry Ghosts: Mao's Secret Famine, *from which this selection was excerpted.*

The prefecture of Xinyang lies in a plain watered by the Huai River. At the time [1958–1961] it was made up of 17 counties and was home to about a fifth of Henan's population of some 50 million. In April 1958, Xinyang shot to fame when the first commune in China was formed within the prefecture at Chayashan in Suiping county. In response to this singular honour, the prefectural Party leadership became fanatically

Jasper Becker, *Hungry Ghosts: Mao's Secret Famine.* New York: The Free Press, 1997. Copyright © 1997 by The Free Press. Reproduced by permission.

devoted to Mao and his dreams and, to sustain them, launched a reign of terror in which tens of thousands were beaten and tortured to death. A Communist Party report published in 1961 described the events not just as mass murder but as 'a holocaust'.

The great terror began in the autumn of 1959 when, in the wake of the Lushan meeting [a 1959 conference at which Mao was warned of impending famine but refused to believe the warning], the prefectural Party committee declared war on the peasants. Those who failed to fulfil their production quotas were condemned as 'little Peng Dehuais' [military commander who openly criticized Mao, later imprisoned] and no mercy was shown towards them. Although the provincial Party Secretary, Wu Zhifu, had lowered the year's grain target for the province in view of a local drought, the zealous Xinyang leadership was determined to show that nature would not be permitted to force a retreat. The leadership insisted that the harvest of 1959 would be as good as that of 1958, so county officials strove to outdo each other in reporting good results. After the summer, the First Secretary of Xinyang prefecture, Lu Xianwen, declared that despite the drought, the 1959 harvest in his region was 3.92 million tonnes, double the real figure. Grain levies, hitherto set at around 30 per cent of the harvest, now amounted in practice to nearly 90 per cent. For example, in one county within the prefecture, Guangshan, cadres reported a harvest of 239,280 tonnes when it was really only 88,392 tonnes, and fixed the grain levy at 75,500 tonnes. When they were unable to collect more than 62,500 tonnes, close to the entire harvest, the local cadres launched a brutal 'anti-hiding campaign'. . . .

Peasants Terrorized

To force the peasants to hand over their last remaining reserves, the officials did not simply beat the peasants but created a nightmare of organized torture and murder. In its unpredictable terror, this rivalled the land reform campaign of 1948. Lu Xianwen issued orders to his cadres to crack down on what he termed 'the three obstacles': people who declared that there was no grain left; peasants who tried to flee; and those who called for the closure of the collective kitchens. In implementing the crackdown, each place invented its own methods of torture. In Guangshan county, local officials thought up thirty different tortures while Huang Chuan county had a list of seventy. Party documents drawn up after the arrest of the Xinyang prefecture's leadership in 1961 give details.

Many involved tying up and beating to death the victims, whose numbers in each locality ran into the hundreds. One Public Security chief, Chen Rubin, personally beat over 200 people in the Yidian production brigade of Dingyuan commune, Luoshan county. Han Defu, Second Secretary of the Segang commune, thrashed over 300 people. Guo Shouli, head of the militia of Nayuan brigade in Liji commune, Gushi county, beat 110 militiamen, 11 of whom were left permanently disabled and 6 of whom died. The same official arrested a commune member, Wei Shaoqiao, who had left one of the dam construction sites and returned home without permission. He was beaten to death, and when his wife came to look for him, she too was tied up and beaten until she died. She was three months pregnant. Guo Shouli then wanted to cut off the 'roots' of the family and killed the couple's 4-year-old child.

Others were buried alive or deliberately frozen to death: 'At the headquarters of the reservoir construction site of Ding Yuan of Luoshan commune, peasant Liu Nanjie had all his clothes removed and was then forced to stand outside in freezing snowy weather' [quote from an unpublished party document]. In another case at Huashudian commune in Guangshan county, thirteen orphans were kept in water outdoors until they all froze to death. A common form of punishment was for cadres to drag people along by their hair. In one case in Huang Chuan county, a peasant woman was dragged for sixty feet over the ground until she died. Officials are also recorded as having tortured people by burning the hair on their heads, chins or genitals. The peasants tried to escape this form of cruelty by shaving off all their hair but then the cadres began to cut off the ears of their victims. . . .

Starvation

Even when, at the start of winter, it was clear that the peasants had nothing to eat but tree bark, wild grass seeds and wild vegetables, Lu Xianwen declared that this was merely 'a ruse of rich peasants' and ordered the search for grain to be redoubled. Party cadres were also incited to smash the cooking pots in every household to prevent them from being used at home to cook grass soup.

Some tried to flee but Lu ordered the arrest of such 'criminals' after seeing children begging by the roadside. Militiamen were instructed to guard every road and railway and to arrest any travellers, even those staying in hostels. All government organizations were given strict orders not to provide refuge to the fleeing peasants. In Gushi county, the militia arrested at least 15,000 people who were then sent to labour camps. In Huang Chuan county, the head of the Public Security Bureau allowed 200 to starve to death in prison and then dispatched the 4 tonnes of grain he had thereby saved to the Party authorities.

The most extraordinary aspect of these events is that throughout the famine the state granaries in the prefecture were full of grain which the peasants said was sufficient to keep everyone alive. Several sources have stated that even at the height of the famine, the Party leadership ate well. By the beginning of 1960, with nothing left to eat and no longer able to flee, the peasants began to die in huge numbers. In the early stages of the famine, most of those who died were old people or men forced to do hard labour on inadequate rations. Now, it was women and children. Whole villages starved to death. In Xixian county alone, 639 villages were left deserted and 100,000 starved to death. A similar number died in Xincai county. Corpses littered the fields and roads as the peasants collapsed from starvation. Few of the bodies were buried. Many simply lay down at home and died.

Cannibalism

That winter, cannibalism became widespread. Generally, the villagers ate the flesh of corpses, especially those of children. In rare cases, parents ate their own children, elder brothers ate younger brothers, elder sisters ate their younger sisters. In most cases, cannibalism was not punished by the Public Security Bureau because it was not considered as severe a crime as destroying state property and the means of production. This latter crime often merited the death sentence. Travelling around the region over thirty years later, every peasant that I met aged over 50 said he personally knew of a case of cannibalism in his production team. One man pointed to a nearby cluster of huts and said he recalled entering a neighbour's house to find him eating the leg of a 5-year-old child of a relative who had died of starvation. The authorities came to hear of what he had done but although he was criticized, he was never put on trial. Generally, though, cannibalism was a secret, furtive event. Women would usually go out at night and cut flesh off the bodies, which lay under a thin layer of soil, and this would then be eaten in secrecy. Sometimes, though, the authorities did intervene. In one commune, a 15-year-old girl who survived by boiling her younger brother's corpse and eating it was caught. The Public Security Bureau charged her with 'destroying a corpse' and put her in prison where she subsequently starved to death. In Gushi county, in 1960, the authorities listed 200 cases of corpses being eaten and charged those arrested with the crime of 'destroying corpses'.

Among the peasants little blame or stigma was apparently attached to breaking such taboos. Bai Hua, one of China's most famous contemporary writers, recalls that while living in another part of China, he heard the following story from a workmate who returned from a visit to Xinyang. There, the man had discovered that all his relatives bar one had starved to death. This was his aunt who had managed to survive through chance because a pig had run into her hut one night. She quickly closed the door, killed it and buried it under the ground. She did not dare share the pork with anyone, not even her 5-year-old son, for she was convinced that if she did so, her son would blurt out the news to the other villagers. Then she feared that the authorities would seize the meat, beat her to death and leave her son to die anyway. So she let him starve to death. Neither Bai Hua nor his workmate condemned the aunt for her actions.

Deaths were kept secret for as long as possible. What food there was was distributed by the collective kitchen and generally one family member would be sent to collect the rations on behalf of the whole household. As long as the death of a family member was kept secret, the rest of the household could benefit from an extra ration. So the corpse would be kept in the hut. In Guangshan county, one woman with three children was caught after she had hidden the corpse of one of them behind the door and then finally, in desperation, had begun to eat it.

The Xinyang prefectural leadership did everything it could to hide what was going on from the world outside. The Party ensured that all mail and telephone calls were monitored and censored. No one could leave the region without written permission from the Party leaders who even posted cadres at the railway station in Zhengzhou, the provincial capital. They were accompanied by guards who searched and usually arrested anyone getting off a train from Xinyang. While in other parts of China the authorities issued starving peasants with 'begging certificates' which allowed them to try their luck elsewhere, this was strictly forbidden in Xinyang. . . .

Mao and the Army

Ultimately, responsibility for what happened in Henan in 1958–61 rested with Mao himself. He had personally sanctioned the orgy of violence and had held up Xinyang as a model for the rest of the country. As early as the beginning of 1959, Mao had received letters from peasants in some counties in Henan protesting that people were starving to death. He disregarded them and in response to complaints that production team leaders were brutally beating peasants who refused to hand over their hidden grain, he addressed a meeting of provincial leaders in February 1959 as follows: 'We should protect the enthusiasm of cadres and working-class people. As for those 5 per cent of cadres who break the law, we should look at them individually, and help them to overcome their mistakes. If we exaggerate this problem it is not good.' Officials were effectively given *carte blanche* to take any measures they wished to seize the fictitious hoards of grain.

However, reports of what was really happening in Henan were reaching the centre, and some influential figures in the capital were becoming concerned. Mao was guarded by a special unit of bodyguards, some of whom were recruited from the Xinyang region which had been an important military base for the Red Amy during the 1940s, and they received letters from their relatives. Another source of information came from inspection tours by Mao's secretary Tian Jiaying and by Chen Yun, one of the most senior figures in the Party. Despite the efforts made to deceive them, both expressed scepticism about Henan's claims. Yet Mao only believed what he wanted to hear. He dismissed reports from these sources and instead accepted as the truth a report from the Xinyang leadership that insisted there was no grain crisis. It admitted that there were problems with falling grain supplies but claimed that this was only due to widespread sabotage by former landlords, counter-revolutionaries, revisionists and feudal elements. The Xinyang Party leadership (who appear to have had a direct channel of communication with Mao) proposed to solve the grain problem with a harsh crackdown. Mao was delighted to hear that, as he had always maintained, class struggle lay behind China's problems. He issued a directive to the rest of the country urging all Party members to deepen the struggle against such class enemies. The Xinyang report was copied and distributed to the whole Party as a model of what was wrong and what should be done about it. To support the Xinyang leadership, he dispatched some members from his own circle to the prefecture in January 1960. According to his doctor, Li Zhisui, Mao sent his confidential secretary, Gao Zhi, and his chief bodyguard, Feng Yaosong. He told them to come back if the assignment became too hard, saying, 'Don't worry, no one will die'.

For the entire summer of 1960 Mao did nothing, although it was by then becoming clear even to him that China was starving. The rest of the Chinese leadership was paralysed, waiting for Mao to change his mind. At the beginning of the winter, inspection teams led by senior Party leaders set out from Beijing to gather evidence of what was going on in the countryside. What happened next in Xinyang is not entirely clear. According to one version, an inspection team led by Chen Yun and Deng Liqun arrived in Xinyang but were detained as they got off the train and confined to a small room. They returned to sound the alarm. Another version has it that an army colonel from Beijing came home on leave and discovered that his relatives in Guangshan county were starving.

Whatever the truth of the matter, the famine was broken in early 1961 when about 30,000 men from the People's Liberation Army (PLA) were ordered to occupy Xinyang, distribute the grain in the state granaries and arrest the prefecture's leadership. The army stayed for three or four months. One source said that in Huang Chuan county, people were so weak they could only crawl across the ground to get to the grain.

Violence in the Cultural Revolution

By Lu Xiuyuan

Mao had become unpopular by the mid-1960s, especially after the debacle of the Great Leap Forward, in which millions died of starvation. Fearful of losing power and still committed to revolutionary principles, in 1966 he initiated what came to be known as the "Great Proletarian Cultural Revolution" (1966–1976). He aligned himself with the most radical political factions and called for an attack on Communist Party members who were not sufficiently "revolutionary" and on all bourgeois elements in Chinese society. Mao encouraged groups of disaffected youth called the Red Guards to quit school, defy all authority, and wander around the country attacking anyone seen as "counterrevolutionary" or a "capitalist roader." A cult grew up around Mao, and Red Guards carried his book of quotations, often called the Little Red Book, with them everywhere.

The Red Guards went after anyone unfortunate enough to be identified as part of the "Four Olds"—old ideas, old cultures, old customs, and old habits. Intellectuals in particular were targeted. Schools closed, and the Red Guards destroyed historic buildings, artifacts, and artworks. Anyone unfortunate enough to be identified as "counterrevolutionary" was humiliated and shamed in public, often savagely beaten and tortured, and forced to do "labor reform." Thousands were murdered, and Chinese society sank into chaos and violence. Even Mao was shocked at the level of violence in the first years of the Cultural Revolution (1966–1968), and he tried to reign in the most radical elements of the Red Guard. It took China ten years to return to some normalcy.

Lu Xiuyuan, who participated in the Cultural Revolution as a high school student in Beijing, was a doctoral candidate in anthropology at Princeton University when she wrote this article describing the violence. She formerly taught at a university in China. Lu Xiuyuan says that when the Cultural Revolution ended, "The Chinese people [had] the common feeling of waking from a dream."

Lu Xiuyuan, "A Step Toward Understanding Popular Violence in China's Cultural Revolution," *Pacific Affairs*, vol. 67, Winter 1994–1995, pp. 533–63. Copyright © 1994 by *Pacific Affairs*. Reproduced by permission.

Although decades have passed [the Cultural Revolution spanned the years 1966 to 1976], the violent scenes of the Cultural Revolution are still so vivid in Chinese memory that it seems as if they happened yesterday, and many Chinese still feel the wounds. Their memories are mainly from the period of 1966–1968, the most random and violent years of the Cultural Revolution.

There was an escalation of violence from 1966 to 1968. Responding to Mao Zedong's call for "Sweeping Away All Monsters and Demons" (*hengsao yiqie niu guei she shen*, class enemies of all descriptions), the campaign of "Destroying the 'Four Olds'" (*po sijiu*, i.e., old ideas, cultures, customs, and habits) raised the cur-

ONE MAN'S STORY OF THE CULTURAL REVOLUTION

An anonymous elementary school teacher describes being arrested and imprisoned during the Cultural Revolution. After ten years in jail, he was finally released when the authorities decided that he had done nothing wrong.

I was interrogated six separate times. Each interrogation was conducted in the middle of the night. They asked me very strange questions. They kept asking me over and over again to turn in my pistol. I thought they must have got it wrong, that it was not me they wanted. I told them, even if you wanted me to go out right now and get a pistol, I wouldn't know where to go to get one. I've spent my whole life in school. When I graduated, I got a job teaching. Except for in the movies, I've never even seen a gun. . . .

I thought that as soon as they figured out that I didn't have any gun, they'd let me go. It had to be a case of mistaken identity, unless someone framed me. But who? I've never been the type to offend people. Who would be so hard-hearted as to set me up? . . .

The interrogator was really patient that day. He said,

tain on the CR mass violence. Thousands of "Red Guards" (*hong weibing*), comprising youths from family backgrounds of "five red types" (*hong wu lei,* i.e., workers, poor and lower-middle-class peasants, revolutionary cadres, revolutionary soldiers, and dependents of revolutionary martyrs), were the protagonists in this social drama. They brought the revolution from the schools into society and brought violence into the ordinary lives of many urban, as well as some rural, people. During the summer of 1966, the "Red Guards" ransacked the homes of the "seven black categories" (*hei qi lei,* i.e., landlords, rich peasants, counterrevolutionaries, evildoers, rightists, capitalists, and reactionary intellectuals) to search for counterrevolutionary evidence and to

"Calm down. Think a little harder. What else do you carry around with you."

I thought again, and then I remembered I'd had a little pistol-shaped ornament on my keychain, about two centimeters long. A friend had given it to me. It was made in France. It was copper inlaid with silver, really pretty. I said, "There was one. A little pendant on my keychain."

The interrogator said, "Exactly. Why didn't you confess to that earlier?"

I was stunned. Had they really thrown me in prison on account of a keychain? . . .

The court pronounced me guilty on three counts: extremely reactionary thought; attacking the command of the proletariat and the policies of the Cultural Revolution; and using my home as a base to receive enemy radio broadcasts, voice grievances on behalf of Liu Shaoqi [president of China at the beginning of the Cultural Revolution, denounced as a "capitalist roader," died in prison in 1969], and plot to organize a counterrevolutionary clique.

Any one of these three crimes was punishable by death. As I drifted in a space of nothingness, I heard them yelling from the stage. "Sentenced to twenty years in prison!"

Anonymous, "I've Become a Different Person," in Feng Jicai, *Ten Years of Madness: Oral Histories of China's Cultural Revolution.* San Francisco: China Books & Periodicals, Inc., 1996, pp. 61–81.

confiscate their property. These "class enemies" were criticized and denounced at public meetings and paraded in the streets bearing humiliating labels. Their hair was cut into various extreme styles by the Red Guards to humiliate them. They were beaten and tortured, and were forced to do physical work as "labor reform" (*laodong gaizao*) in the cities or were sent to the countryside. Many were killed by abuse and violence. In some of the worst areas of the countryside, not only the "class enemies" themselves but also their family members were executed. Within the climate of "Red Terror," many people resorted to suicide to avoid the torture and killing. Suicide was called "dreading punishment for one's crime" and "alienating oneself from the people," but by giving up their lives, these suicides showed their resistance to the inhumane physical and spiritual treatment so many were forced to undergo.

Numerous ancient sites and historical relics were damaged due to being "Four Olds." Churches and abbeys were attacked, and the nuns and monks were expelled. The old names of streets, schools, department stores, and product brands were changed to revolutionary ones; for example, Yangwei ("raise power/prestige") Road, where the Russian embassy was located, was renamed Fanxiu ("Anti-revisionism") Road. "Bourgeois tastes" were also included within the scope of "sweeping away." "Bourgeois bizarre attire" (*zichanjieji qi zhuang yi fu*), such as close-fitting or wide trouser legs, pointed-toe or high-heeled shoes, or long hair, were attacked. People in such attire not only were stopped on the streets and criticized, but also often were "revolutionized"—the high heels or pointed toes of shoes were cut off; trousers were destroyed with scissors; long hair was clipped on the streets or in barber shops. The ordinary lives of numerous Chinese people were threatened and disrupted.

But the most important enemies, the focus of the CR, as Mao said, were those in power who were taking the capitalist road, namely, the "capitalist roaders" (*zou zi pai*). They were leaders on many different levels. Through denouncing the "Work Teams" and party organizations that tried to control order by nailing new "rightists" and through annulling the black materials they put in people's dossiers, as well as through attacking the "blood pedigree theory" (*xuetonglun*), the campaign "Criticizing the Bourgeois Reactionary Line" (*pipan zichanjieji fandong luxian*) mobilized a broad cross section of people, especially those of "grey" and "black" family origins, to join the struggle against the "capitalist roaders." The "capitalist roaders" were treated just like the "old enemies," and the attacks on them drew more ordinary Chinese into the violence. This policy was surprising and extremely difficult to accept by people who had long represented the revolution and who had criticized others. I think it is likely that, as a Western journalist claims, the suicide rate among these ex-bourgeois leaders was much higher than that of "old enemies" during the initial eruption of the CR.

From 1967 to 1968, there was a long period of "fighting between factions" (*paixing douzheng* or *da paizhang*). In contrast to the situation at the beginning of the CR, after 1966 most people could join the Red Guards, previously a privilege of the "five red types." Red Guards within each city or unit divided themselves into two opposing groups, often called the "rebel faction" (*zaofan pai*) and the "conservative faction" (*baoshou pai* or *baohuang pai*). They debated and fought not only orally and in writing, but soon also with sticks, fragments of bricks, and finally guns. More and more people died in the fighting. Additionally, during the early half of 1968, often backed by military officials, conservative groups launched a crucial suppression of the rebels all over the country. The better-situated the conservatives were, the worse the suppression was. In the worst provinces of Guangxi and Guangdong, leaders of rebel groups were arrested, paraded, humiliated, and then killed or maimed. "The United Headquarters of Proletarian Revolutionary Factions" in Guangxi killed their counterpart student rebels of the "April 22 Group" in a mass execution after their surrender or capture. Accused as behind-the-scene supporters of the rebels, "class enemies" and their offspring were executed in large-scale and extremely brutal ways. The most barbaric cannibalism—eating enemies—was done in Guangxi as the way to demonstrate intense "class feeling."

How many people died during the Cultural Revolution? Estimates vary from one million to twenty million. In Guangxi province, based on Zheng Yi's field research, the "unnatural deaths" during the CR are officially estimated at ninety-thousand but are said among the populace to be at least twice that number. According to national officials, about one hundred million people (one-tenth of the country's population) suffered during the CR. Regardless of the precise numbers, it is certain that the trauma and impact on the Chinese people as a whole was immense.

One Dissident Speaks Out for Democracy

BY WEI JINGSHENG

A new democracy movement appeared in China following the Cultural Revolution. In 1978, posters criticizing the government began appearing on "Democracy Wall," a wall on a street in Beijing where, for a short time, authorities allowed individuals to post political posters. One of the leaders of the democracy movement was Wei Jingsheng. Wei called for a "fifth modernization"—democracy—as a response to Chinese premiere Zhou Enlai's four economic modernizations in agriculture, industry, defense, and science. By 1979 the authorities began to criticize leaders of the Democracy Wall movement as being too "individualistic." Wei was arrested just before the government imposed restrictions on the movement. He was tried and convicted of "counterrevolutionary" crimes and sentenced to die. His sentence was commuted to fifteen years in prison after he had already spent eight months on death row. Wei was released from jail briefly in 1993, then re-arrested and sent back to prison, but by that time he was China's most prominent dissident. In 1997 the government released him from jail and forced him to leave the country.

In these excerpts from his essay "Democracy or a New Dictatorship?" Wei bluntly criticizes the Chinese authorities and calls for democratic reform. This essay was first published in 1979 in the Chinese journal Exploration. *Wei Jingsheng's letters from prison appeared under the title* The Courage to Stand Alone.

Everyone in China knows that the Chinese social system is not democratic and that this lack of democracy has severely stunted every aspect of the country's social development over the past thirty years. In the face of this hard fact there are two choices before the Chinese people. Either to reform the social system if they want to develop their society and seek a swift increase in prosperity and economic resources; or, if they are content with a continuation of the Mao Zedong brand of proletarian dictatorship, then they cannot even talk of democracy, nor will they be able to realize the modernization of their lives and resources.

Where is China heading and in what sort of society do the people hope to live and work?

The answer can be seen in the mood of the majority. It is this mood that brought about the present democratic movement. With the denial of Mao Zedong's style of dictatorship as its very prerequisite, the aim of this movement is to reform the social system and thereby enable the Chinese people to increase production and develop their lives to the full in a democratic social environment. This aim is not just the aim of a few isolated individuals but represents a whole trend in the development of Chinese society. . . .

The people want to appeal against injustice, want to vent their grievances, and want democracy, so they hold meetings. The people oppose famine and dictatorship, so they demonstrate. This shows that without democracy their very livelihood lacks any safeguard. Is it possible, when the people are so much at the mercy of others, that such a situation can be called "normal public order"? If "normal public order" gives dictators the right to wreak havoc with the people's interests, then does it benefit the careerists or the people to safeguard such an order? Is the answer not painfully obvious? We consider that normal public order is not total uniformity; particularly in politics, where there must be a great diversity of opinion. When there are no divergent opinions, no discussion, and no publications, then it is clear that there is a dictatorship. Total uniformity must surely be called "abnormal order." When social phenomena are interpreted as the occasion for criminal elements to make trouble and are used as an excuse to do away with the people's right to express their opinions, this is the time-honored practice of fascist dictators both new and old. . . .

So the crux of the matter is not who becomes master of the nation, but rather that the people must maintain firm control over their own nation, for this is the very essence of democracy. People entrusted with government positions must be controlled by and responsible to the people. According to the Constitution, organizations and individuals in the administration must be elected by the people, empowered and controlled by an elected government under the supervision of the people, and responsible to the people; only then is there a legality for executive powers.

We would like to ask the high officials who instigate the arrest of individuals—is the power you exercise legal? We would like to ask Chairman Hua Guofeng and Vice-Chairman Deng Xiaoping—is your occupation of the highest offices of state legal? We would like to know why it is the Vice-Chairman and the Vice-Premier and not the courts or organizations representing the people who announce who is to be arrested. Is this legal? According to Chinese law, is a "bad element" a criminal per se? And on whose judgment is such a criterion made? If these simple questions are not clearly answered there is no point in talking about rule by law in China. . . .

Furthering reforms within the social system and moving Chinese politics toward democracy are prerequisites for solving the social and economic problems that confront China today. Only through elections can the leadership gain the people's voluntary cooperation and bring their initiative into play. Only when the people enjoy complete freedom and expression can they help their leaders to analyze and solve problems. Cooperation, together with policies formulated and carried out by the people, are necessary for the highest degree of working efficiency and the achievement of ideal results.

This is the only road along which China can make progress. Under present-day conditions, it is an extremely difficult path.

Deng Xiaoping Opens China to the World

By Roderick MacFarquhar

Deng Xiaoping (1904–1997) was purged twice in the Cultural Revolution and rehabilitated twice. When Deng came into power in the late 1970s, he was determined to open his country to the world and to revolutionize the Chinese economy. "To get rich is glorious," Deng declared, and the Chinese people responded. His economic reforms made real improvements in the standard of living for the average Chinese citizen. Deng is also responsible for putting in place the one-child policy, which forbids most couples from producing more than one child.

Deng's reforms affected the political system but did not significantly change it. He advocated "opening up" and allowed foreign ideas and influences into China, but he left the one-party structure in place, and he severely enforced limits on political expression. Deng will be remembered just as much for his brutal suppression of the 1989 Student Democracy Movement in Beijing's Tiananmen Square as for his economic policies.

Roderick MacFarquhar, Leroy B. Williams Professor of History and Political Science at Harvard University, reviews Deng's accomplishments and shortcomings in the following excerpt. MacFarquhar is the author of numerous books on China, including the three-volume work The Origins of the Cultural Revolution.

D eng Xiaoping was eulogized by his colleagues as the "chief architect" of China's reform program and its opening to the outside world. This was misleading. Deng was no master builder. Unlike his patron, Mao Zedong, and fortunately for his countrymen, he had no utopian blueprints for the future, except perhaps the century-old dream of Chinese states-

Roderick MacFarquhar, "Demolition Man," *New York Review of Books*, vol. XLIV, March 27, 1997, pp. 14–17. Copyright © 1997 by the *New York Review of Books*. Reproduced by permission.

men that China must become rich and powerful. But, like Mao, he was a demolition man. Deng deconstructed the China he took over: not the traditional China of Confucian values and Taoist cults, but the China of Communist principles and practices which he had himself helped Mao to superimpose upon their land.

When Deng took over in December 1978, "China was faced with a very grim situation and extremely arduous tasks. It was imperative to break away from the calamities caused by the 'Great Cultural Revolution.'" All agreed on that, but most of Deng's surviving peers were nostalgic for the "golden age" of the 1950s, the Soviet model redux but reshaped. Deng forced them to go in the opposite direction.

Mao had always talked a good line about "liberating" the people, but insisted they obey his vision. "Liberation" is used by the Chinese Communists to describe the revolution of 1949, after which they put the people in a Leninist straitjacket. During the past seventeen years, Deng did actually liberate the Chinese people from Stalinist economics and Maoist social theory, enabling them to prosper as never before. He shrank from abandoning Leninist politics as well—after the chaos of the Cultural Revolution, he felt it was China's only guarantee of stability—but his reforms have also undermined that system, as the events in Tiananmen Square in 1989 demonstrated. . . .

Deng the True Revolutionary

Deng was a true revolutionary, as he himself recognized: "We too say that what we are doing now is in essence a revolution," he told Mike Wallace in 1986. Deng returned China to the path of seeking wealth and power, but he was not simply another "self-strengthener" like the great mandarins of the latter half of the nineteenth century. Unlike them, he made historic breaks with China's past in order to set the country on a path of rapid modernization.

History should deal more kindly with Deng than with Mao, who increasingly seems a transitional and traditional figure. Mao won a civil war, reunited the country, rebuilt the strong central state, and restored the respect of foreign powers, but so did many founding emperors to whom Chinese often compared him. Unlike other founders, Mao would not make the transition from revolutionary to ruler. Mao was a rebel with a cause, whose lethal egalitarianism lasted twenty years, cost millions of lives, and fatally crippled the regime he had set up. He sought utopia, but China almost ended up in a state of nature.

Deng became Mao's protégé when still in his twenties, and displayed great talent in party organization and on the battlefield. He was a quick study and a decisive leader, a doer not a dreamer like Mao, a pragmatist not a theoretician like Liu Shaoqi. After the revolution, his loyalty and abilities were rewarded when he became General Secretary of the Party. In that role, he energetically supported Mao's Anti-Rightist Campaign against the intellectuals and the disastrous Great Leap Forward. The catastrophe sobered him into advocating policies that Mao found suspect, and so Deng became a principal victim of the Cultural Revolution. Yet when Zhou Enlai [premiere and foreign minister of China] was dying, and Mao needed someone with the self-confident authority to run the state and to discipline the People's Liberation Army, his only choice was to recall Deng. Deng attempted to stem the Cultural Revolution and was purged again one last time, but this made him the Chairman's inevitable successor, the only man of his generation admired by Mao and his victims alike.

A Strategy of Liberation

The timing of Deng's return to power at the end of 1978 was critical. When the Cultural Revolution started in 1966, there were only three models of modernization to choose from: the Western, which was unacceptable, the Soviet, which had been found wanting, and the Maoist, which had proved calamitous. Twelve years later, Japan and the four little dragons—Korea, Taiwan, Singapore, and Hong Kong—three of them peopled by Chinese, had transformed East Asia into an economic powerhouse: they had found not only a route to wealth and power, but one that was almost indigenous, certainly within the old Chinese cultural sphere. Deng adopted and adapted the East Asian model.

Deng launched a late Qing-style great leap, unleashing forces rather than mobilizing them. From the Hundred Flowers episodes of 1957 and 1961, he had learned that intellectuals, while often critical, were willing to devote their talents to the good of the nation if given the chance. From the Great Leap Forward, he had learned that the more effective the mass mobilization, the more horrendous the disaster. In the early 1960s, he had learned that the way to transform agriculture, the Achilles heel of Chinese development, was not to dragoon the peasants but to liberate them, a measure which no previous reform program, Qing, Nationalist, or Maoist, had envisaged. Deng seems first to have announced his anti-collectivist formula. "It doesn't matter if a cat is black or white, so long as it catches the mouse it's a good cat," at a meeting of the party secretariat in June 1962: but it was plagiarized from the peasants. Briefly in the early 1960s, he saw too that Chinese entrepreneurship was not dead, it also just had to be liberated. And the Cultural Revolution had proved to him that an inward-looking China, cut off from the outside world, would never progress.

Deng never formulated a clear vision of China's future, but once in command he certainly had a clear idea of how to get there, wherever or whatever it was: "It's the economy stupid." For Deng, liberation of the economy, from the shackles of central planning and the shibboleths of socialism, making "practice the sole criterion of truth," was the key to the success of what he vaguely called "building socialism with Chinese characteristics." Deng's reform program has been lustier than all its predecessors precisely because he was prepared to set people free to improve their lot as they saw fit rather than forced them to conform to some grandiose vision of his own.

Relaxing the Grip

Deng's reforms involved historic changes in the conduct of the Chinese state. "To get rich is glorious" sounds crass, but for the first time in Chinese history, profit is not a dirty word. Long before Communist cadres came along, Confucian mandarins sought to constrain private wealth, whose power they distrusted. The commanding heights of the economy had to be in government hands, be it salt and iron under the Han or oil and steel in the PRC [People's Republic of China]. But Deng had decided that a command economy would not take off. Government did not know best. China had to grow out of the plan. He failed to solve the problem of the money-losing state-owned enterprises (SOEs), whose debts are an ongoing threat to the health of the banking system. Putting hundreds of thousands of angry workers on the street was politically unfeasible. That problem he has left for heirs to solve.

Deng also relaxed the political grip of the central state apparatus. Ever since the Sui dynasty reinstituted the Chinese impe-

rial system in the sixth century AD, after three centuries of disunity, the prime aim of Chinese statecraft has been to keep the
country in one piece by strong central control. Under communism, the powers of modern media and organization greatly facilitated the Party's ability to perform that role. Deng broke with
tradition. To allow some regions to get rich first, Deng devolved
power in an unprecedented manner which could be described as
"economic federalism." This left some regions very poor, but it
also made sense for his announced policy of "one country, two
systems." If Hong Kong and Taiwan witnessed devolution working for Guangdong or Shanghai, they might be more reassured
of its working for them too.

Thirdly, Deng's policy of *kaifang*—"opening up"—has made
the country accessible to foreign ideas and influences in a manner unprecedented since the Tang dynasty in the seventh century
AD, and to a degree far greater than during the Tang. Deng sym-
bolically reaffirmed the policy on his deathbed. In 1976, Zhou
Enlai had asked that his ashes be "scattered in the rivers and on
the land of our motherland." Deng chose the sea. Since he apparently talked a lot about his funeral arrangements, his choice
was not a casual one. His idea of a last resting place was surely a
metaphor for his reform program. In the late 1980s, Deng's conservative colleagues were incensed by the TV documentary series "River Elegy" (*He Shang*), in which the Yellow River stood
for the inward-looking traditional culture that had kept China
backward, while the blue ocean stood for the global culture
which China had to join if it wished to modernize. In life, Deng
cast the deciding vote for *kaifang*. In death, he underlined that
part of his legacy for his successors.

Political Repression

Despite the revolutionary nature of his program, and the importance of his legacy, Deng's record is deeply flawed by the massacre in Tiananmen Square on June 4, 1989. So notorious is the
suppression of the students' democracy movement in China that
it is commonly referred to simply as "6.4," *liu si*, June 4. Only
one other date in modern Chinese history could be referred to
in this abbreviated manner without confusion: "5.4," *wu si*, May
4, the date of an anti-imperialism student demonstration in Beijing in 1919, which thereafter became the name for a widespread
movement of national renewal. The Chinese Communist Party,

founded in 1921, claims its origins in the womb of the May Fourth Movement, and the two dates serve as convenient bookends of the idealistic promise of the Chinese revolution.

"May Fourth" and "June Fourth" stand for periods of widespread yearning, searches for better futures than the national disunity and warlordism succeeding the 1911 revolution, and the political, economic, and human disasters that were the product of the 1949 one. Both movements were broadly in favor of democracy and against the corrupt political and social systems of the day. The two movements were spearheaded by intellectuals and students— *"Bliss was it in that dawn to be alive/But to be young was very Heaven!"*—with the students bearing the brunt of the struggle during the "incidents" themselves. That the educated elite represented the feelings and aspirations, however inchoate, of large sections of urban China during both movements is shown by the enthusiastic support they generated throughout the country. . . .

Deng's determination to "seek truth from facts," his pragmatic willingness to do whatever it took to transform China economically, was refreshing when contrasted with the more hide-bound attitudes of many of his peers and predecessors. But his neglect of any larger vision endangered his project. Like the late-nineteenth-century mandarins, he was hobbled by an abiding faith in the rightness of the prevailing political system, and in its durability so long as the economy could be developed. Like them, he mistakenly thought he could adopt Western learning for the purposes of modernization while preserving the political essence of the Chinese state. Western technology seemed like something peripheral that could be plugged into any political hardware. Like them, he failed to realize that the intellectual milieu in which such technology can be elaborated is an integral part of an open political operating system. You cannot travel far down the information superhighway in the political equivalent of a Model T.

The manner of the Qing dynasty collapse should have instructed Deng in the peril of simultaneously launching radical economic, intellectual, and social reform programs with serious political implications—especially if those programs effectively abandon their overall ideological justification, thus undermining the legitimacy and status of the bureaucratic class that has been the regime's strongest supporter. Deng did not even need a knowledge of history, for his conservative colleagues were constantly warning him of the danger, and in April–June 1989 they proved prophetic.

Deng saved the day then with the help of the military, but the collapse of the Soviet Union at the end of 1991 underlined the Qing lesson by demonstrating that once-powerful regimes based on total control could disappear overnight, even without defeat in major war. Deng went off early in 1992 on a southern tour to show his support for the booming new economic zones and to reinvigorate the reforms; but he could not restore the world Communist movement, the system of which China had once proudly been a part, the future that had not worked. The once-legitimizing creed of Marxism–Leninism–Mao Zedong Thought is styled a cardinal principle in Beijing, but it has few Chinese adherents, probably not even Deng in his last years. Since the disappearance of communism in the Soviet Union and Eastern Europe, question marks have hovered over China's political future for Deng's heirs to try to answer.

The Tiananmen Square Massacre

By Jonathan D. Spence

Although many events have been held in Beijing's Tiananmen Square, none is more infamous than the brutal suppression of the student democracy movement there in 1989. In this selection from his book The Search for Modern China, *eminent Sinologist Jonathan D. Spence recounts the intellectual and political climate of the times, the origin and goals of the student reform movement, the Communist Party's response, and the final, violent suppression in the early morning hours of June 4. Spence is George Burton Adams Professor of History at Yale University and author of numerous works on China, including* The Gate of Heavenly Peace *and* Emperor of China: Self-Portrait of K'ang-hsi.

Nineteen eighty-nine promised to be an anniversary year of special significance for China: the year would mark the two hundredth anniversary of the French Revolution, the seventieth anniversary of the May Fourth movement [a nationalistic movement of 1919], the fortieth birthday of the People's Republic itself, and the passage of ten years since formal diplomatic relations with the United States had been reinstituted. A number of China's most prominent scientists and writers—including the dismissed party member Fang Lizhi and the poet Bei Dao—sent letters to Deng Xiaoping and other leaders asking them to seize this opportune moment to take steps that would emphasize the flexibility and openness of Chinese politics. They urged that Wei Jingsheng, who had now served ten years in prison for his role in the 1978 Democracy Wall movement [movement calling for political reform], be granted amnesty, along with others who were in prison solely for their dissident political views. They also urged the government to grant the rights of freedom of expression that would allow the kind of lively intellectual exchange considered essential to real scientific and economic progress, and to put more money into education for the sake of the country as a whole. Delegates to the National People's Congress suggested that a "socialist democracy" promised a solution if it could combine "political, social and cultural democratization" with the economic reform currently under discussion. Other intellectuals urged a return to the kind of pragmatism that had seemed to be implied by Deng Xiaoping's famous remark from the late 1970s: "It does not matter whether a cat is black or white: as long as it catches mice it is a good cat." Others went further, like the former head of the Marxism–Leninism–Mao Zedong Thought Institute, Su Shaozhi, who suggested that the divorce between theory and practice was now a "chronic malady" in China. Echoing the disgraced party secretary-general Hu Yaobang, he pointed out that Marxism in China currently seemed frozen in the grip of "ossified dogmas." Surely genuine reform could invigorate Marxism while rejecting all "ideological prejudices and bureaucratism," all "cultural autocracy."

Such voices were a reaffirmation of what the massed students in Hefei had called for in 1986 [student demonstrations calling for political reform], and of what Wei Jingsheng had himself boldly suggested in 1978 and 1979: without abandoning the spirit of Marxism itself, there was still room for creative growth and change. Neither Deng Xiaoping, Li Peng [member of Central Committee and Politburo], or Zhao Ziyang [general secretary of Communist Party] responded publicly to these various overtures, leaving the task to their subordinates, whose response was harshly dismissive. Such requests and critiques, they observed, were "incitements" to the public and an attempt to exert "pressure" on the government. Since there were no political prisoners in China, the request to "release" Wei Jingsheng and others was a meaningless one.

The Demonstrations Begin

In this uneasy atmosphere, on April 15, 1989, Hu Yaobang suddenly died of a heart attack. Hu, the feisty Long March [Communist march to escape Nationalist troops, 1934] veteran and Communist Youth League leader, had been Deng Xiaoping's handpicked secretary-general of the CCP [Chinese Communist Party] until he was made the scapegoat for allowing the 1986–

1987 student demonstrations to spread. At the time of his dismissal from his party posts in 1987 the Central Committee had made him issue a humiliating "self-criticism"; the nature of this disgrace and the way Deng condoned or even encouraged it had left a bad taste in Chinese mouths. As soon as the news of Hu Yaobang's death was released, students in Peking saw a means of pressuring the government to move more vigorously with economic and democratic reforms. It was Deng Xiaoping, after all, who in 1978 had "reversed the verdicts" on the Tiananmen

DENG XIAOPING'S REASONS FOR SENDING IN TROOPS

On June 2, 1989, top leaders of the Chinese Communist Party met and discussed the Tiananmen Square student demonstrations. Deng Xiaoping's comments indicated that he blamed the West for the demonstrations, and he feared that civil war would ensue if they were allowed to continue.

"The causes of this incident have to do with the global context. The Western world, especially the United States, has thrown its entire propaganda machine into agitation work and has given a lot of encouragement and assistance to the so-called democrats or opposition in China—people who in fact are the scum of the Chinese nation. This is the root of the chaotic situation we face today. When the West stirs up turmoil in other countries, in fact it is playing power politics—hegemonism—and is only trying to control those other countries, to pull into its power sphere countries that were previously beyond its control. . . . Some Western countries use things like 'human rights,' or like saying the socialist system is irrational or illegal, to criticize us, but what they're really after is our sovereignty. Those Western countries that play power politics have no right at all to talk about human rights! Look how many people around the world they've robbed of human rights! And look how many Chi-

demonstrations of 1976 in homage to the deceased Zhou Enlai, thus openly acknowledging the legitimacy of such actions. By launching a pro-Hu Yaobang demonstration, and demanding a reversal of the verdict against him too, the students would ensure that all the issues of the 1986–1987 pro-democracy protests, and perhaps also those of Democracy Wall in 1978–1979, would once more be at the forefront of the nation's attention.

This idea seems to have originated with students in the party-history department at People's University in Peking [Beijing].

---

nese people they've hurt the human rights of since they invaded China during the Opium War! . . .

"Imagine for a moment what could happen if China falls into turmoil. If it happens now, it'd be far worse than the Cultural Revolution. Back then the prestige of the old generation of leaders like Chairman Mao and Premier Zhou still loomed. We talked about 'full-scale civil war,' but actually no large-scale fighting took place, no true civil war ever happened. Now it's different, though. If the turmoil keeps going, it could continue until Party and state authority are worn away. Then there would be civil war, one faction controlling parts of the army and another faction controlling others. If the so-called democracy fighters were in power, they'd fight among themselves. Once civil war got started, blood would flow like a river, and where would human rights be then? In a civil war, each power would dominate a locality, production would fall, communications would be cut off, and refugees would flow out of China not in millions or tens of millions but in hundreds of millions. First hit by this flood of refugees would be Pacific Asia, which is currently the most promising region of the world. This would be disaster on a global scale. So China mustn't make a mess of itself. And this is not just to be responsible to ourselves, but to consider the whole world and all of humanity as well."

Deng Xiaoping, excerpt from meeting on June 2, 1989, quoted in Zhang Liang, compiler, Andrew J. Nathan and Perry Link, eds., *The Tiananmen Papers*. New York: Public Affairs, 2001, pp. 158, 159.

Many of these students were themselves party members and the children of senior Communist cadres, and could be expected soon to be embarking on careers in the party bureaucracy or the new economic corporations. They understood how to apply political pressure and how to maintain it. Thousands of students from the other Peking campuses, including Peking University [Beijing University or Beida] itself, joined them in a rally that was held in Tiananmen Square on April 17. Their purpose was to mourn Hu's passing and to call for an end to corruption and nepotism in government, for more democratic participation in decision making, and for better conditions in the universities. Wall posters—declared illegal by the party since 1980—appeared in many places, openly praising Hu and his support of liberalism and political and economic reform. After class, and when the libraries closed, excited groups of young people would join together spontaneously and share their feelings; from such gatherings sprang new, autonomous student associations. Students in Shanghai and other cities caught the mood and took up the same cry. On April 18, students held a sit-in near the Great Hall of the People in Tiananmen Square: that night, with bravado unparalleled under the PRC, they staged sit-ins at the party headquarters and in front of the most senior party leaders' residences in the Zhongnanhai compound on the edge of the Forbidden City. The government declared April 22 to be the official day for Hu Yaobang's funeral ceremonies; demonstrations were forbidden and plans made to cordon off the whole of Tiananmen Square. But by clever preparation and inspired coordination, Peking students entered the square before the police had taken up their positions and held a large, peaceful demonstration. In a ritualistic but sincere gesture, reminiscent of Qing practice, several students knelt on the steps of the Great Hall and begged Premier Li Peng to come out and talk to them. He declined to do so. On April 24, students began a mass boycott of classes in an attempt to pressure government leaders into hearing their requests.

The Protests Grow

Up to this point, compromise of many kinds appeared possible, even if the demonstrators had gone beyond anything attempted in 1976, 1978, or 1986. Zhao Ziyang was believed by students to be receptive to dialogue over changes, as were many of his senior staff, and in his position as secretary-general of the CCP he could presumably urge the party in the same direction. Zhao, for his part, may have seen the students' demonstrations as a potential political force that could strengthen his own party base and enable him to shunt aside Li Peng and perhaps even Deng Xiaoping himself. (In 1978 Deng Xiaoping had successfully used the Democracy Wall protests to cement his position against Hua Guofeng.) But in late April the students and their supporters were stunned by a strong editorial in *People's Daily* that referred to their movement as a "planned conspiracy," firmly implying that all those following the current action might be subject to arrest and prosecution. Zhao himself was away on a state visit to North Korea at the time, and the *People's Daily* editorial obviously represented the views of a tougher group of party leaders, perhaps Premier Li Peng or Deng Xiaoping himself.

Instead of being intimidated, the students reacted with anger and defiance. They were joined now by many of their teachers, by scores of journalists, and by citizens of Peking. The rallies and marches grew larger, the calls for reforms and democratic freedoms more bold. The government leaders appeared paralyzed, for any use of force on the anniversary of the May Fourth demonstrations would immediately lead to reminders of the warlord era. May 4 came and went peaceably, though over 100,000 marched in Peking, dwarfing the student demonstrations of 1919. Similar rallies and parades were held in cities throughout China, but it was Peking that remained the focus for world media attention, not only because of the demonstrations, but because the secretary-general of the Soviet Communist party, Mikhail Gorbachev, was due in Peking in mid-May for a crucial and long-planned summit meeting with Deng Xiaoping. This summit was expected to mark the end of the rift between the Soviet Union and China that had lasted for thirty-three years, ever since Khrushchev had shocked Mao with his "secret speech" attacking Stalin's memory.

Hunger Strike

Gorbachev was enthusiastically welcomed by the Peking demonstrators, not least because his own attempts to introduce a range of new political and intellectual freedoms in the Soviet Union could be contrasted sharply with the Chinese leaders' obvious resistance to such change. But the significance of Gorbachev's visit and the benign light this might have cast on Deng Xiaoping was overshadowed as the student demonstrators introduced a new tactic—the hunger strike—to emphasize their pleas for reform. Tiananmen Square became a vast camp as close to 3,000 hunger strikers lay out in makeshift tents, surrounded by tens of thousands of their classmates. Peking citizens, and curious visitors and onlookers. Students all over Peking were kept in touch with the latest developments by a squad of volunteer motorcyclists who

EYEWITNESS TO THE MASSACRE

Canadian journalist Jan Wong observed the Tiananmen Square massacre from a hotel balcony overlooking the square and recorded the horrifying things she saw that night.

Norman [Wong's husband] and I had left the square in the nick of time. Ten minutes later, the troops rolled in from the west side, the armored personnel carriers roaring easily over makeshift barricades. Protesters hurled stones. A cyclist gave impotent chase. I could hear the crackle of gunfire clearly now. I watched in horror as the army shot directly into the crowds, who stampeded screaming and cursing down the Avenue of Eternal Peace. At first, some protesters held blankets and jackets in front of them, apparently believing the army was using rubber bullets. Only after the first people fell, with gaping wounds, did people comprehend that the soldiers were using live ammunition. . . .

A crowd below frantically tried to rip down a metal fence to erect another barricade. When it wouldn't budge, they smashed a window of a parked bus, put the gears in neutral and rolled it onto the street. They did that with a second and then a third bus. The rest of the crowd shouted, "*Hao!*" ("Good!").

The troops and tanks began closing in from all directions. At 1:20, I heard bursts of gunfire from the south, then another burst five minutes later. At 2:10, several thousand troops marched across the north side of the square. At 2:15, they raised their guns and fired into the dense crowd. I

proudly named themselves the "Flying Tigers." Planned ceremonies for Gorbachev had to be canceled or changed by the
Chinese government, and as television cameras broadcast the
scene around the world, ambulances raced in and out of the
square attending to those now so dangerously weakened by their
fast that there was a real chance they would die.

Nothing like this had been seen in China before, for although

timed the murderous volley on my watch. It lasted more
than a minute. Although the square was brightly lit, the
streets surrounding it were dark. I couldn't see clearly if anyone had been hit. I assumed they must have been because of
the angle of the guns, the length of the volley and the den-
sity of the crowds. A few minutes later I knew I was right
as five ambulances raced by the hotel through the crowds.
Cyclists and pedicab drivers helped evacuate the wounded
and dying. . . .

In the darkness I could make out a double row of soldiers, approximately one hundred and twenty men across. At
2:35, they began firing into the crowds as they marched
across the square. With each volley, tens of thousands of
people fled toward the hotel. Someone commandeered a
bus, drove it toward the soldiers and was killed in a hail of
gunfire. The crowd began to scream, "Go back! Go back!"
The soldiers responded with another hail of bullets. . . .

The soldiers strafed ambulances and shot medical workers trying to rescue the wounded. Some cyclists flung bodies across the back of their bicycles. Others just carried the
wounded on their backs. Beijing's doughty pedicab drivers
pitched in. Between 3:15 and 3:23, I counted eighteen pedi-
cabs pass by me carrying the dead and wounded to the
nearby Beijing Hospital, diagonally across from the hotel, or
to the nearby Beijing Union Medical Hospital. I realized that
I had seen the same driver in a red undershirt several times.
The straw matting on his cart was soaked with blood.

Jan Wong, *Red China Blues: My Long March from Mao to Now.* Toronto:
Doubleday/Anchor Books, 1996, pp. 251–54.

crowds as large had assembled during the Cultural Revolution, those gatherings had been orchestrated by the state and were held in homage to Mao Zedong as supreme leader of the party and the people. Now, even though Zhao Ziyang still tried to mute the conflict, and suggested that the *People's Daily's* condemnation of the students had been too harsh, the demonstrators began openly calling on Deng Xiaoping and Li Peng to resign. Boisterous and angry, sometimes chanting and dancing, at other times deep in political discussion or sleeping in exhaustion, the students and their supporters were at once a potent political challenge to their government and an endlessly engrossing spectacle to the rest of China and the world. Li Peng did invite the hunger-strike leaders to one meeting, but it went badly [the student leaders were Wuer Kaixi, who escaped to Hong Kong and the West after the crackdown, and Wang Dan, who was caught and imprisoned]. Li found the students rude and incoherent, while they found him arrogant and aloof. On May 17 and again the following day, the number of demonstrators in and around Tiananmen Square passed the 1 million mark. Muzzled until now by government controls, journalists and editors of newspapers and television news threw off their restraints and began to cover the protests as honestly and comprehensively as they could. On May 19, appearing close to tears, Secretary-General Zhao Ziyang visited the hunger strikers and urged them to end their fasts. Li Peng also briefly talked with strikers, but made no pleas and no promises. On May 20, with no published comment by Zhao Ziyang, Premier Li Peng and the president of China, Yang Shangkun, declared martial law and ordered units of the People's Liberation Army (PLA) brought into Peking to clear the square and return order to the city.

But for two weeks the soldiers could not clear the square, their efforts stymied by the courage and unity of the citizens of Peking. Workers, initially sought out as allies by the students, now organized themselves into their own groups to join in the protests and to stem the soldiers' advance. With a kind of fierce yet loving solidarity, the people of Peking took to the streets and erected makeshift barricades. They surrounded the army convoys, sometimes to let the air out of tires or stall engines but more often to argue with or cajole the troops, urging them not to enforce the martial-law restrictions and not to turn their guns on their fellow Chinese. For their part the troops, seemingly embarrassed by their assignment, practiced considerable restraint while the central leadership of China, both in the party and the army, was clearly divided. Enraged by the students' intransigence and the mounting disorder in the streets, which surely reminded him of the Cultural Revolution, Deng Xiaoping lobbied for hard-line support and ordered each of the regional PLA commanders to send a certain number of their seasoned troops to the capital. Zhao Ziyang found himself without a sufficient base of support among his colleagues, and was unable to check the hard-line approach from gaining ground.

The students who had emerged as leaders of the demonstrations over the previous month now found themselves in charge of a huge square crammed with their supporters but also awash with dirt and garbage that threatened the outbreak of serious disease. At May's end they began to urge their fellow students to end the hunger strikes, return to their campuses, and continue to attempt a dialogue with the government from there, and the great majority of the Peking students did so. But there were new recruits—often from other cities where major demonstrations were occurring—to take their place. Speakers espousing a tougher stance urged that retreat would mean a betrayal of their principles, and that the government would never speak to them openly unless they maintained the pressures they were currently exerting through their numbers and tenacity. A group of Peking art students provided the faltering movement with a new symbol that drew all eyes—a thirty-foot-high white plaster and Styrofoam statue of their version of Liberty, fashioned as a young woman with head held proudly aloft, clasping in both her hands the torch of freedom.

The Army Moves In

Late at night on June 3, the army struck. These were not inexperienced and poorly armed soldiers like those called in up to this time, but tough, well-armed troops from the Twenty-seventh Army (whose commander was a relative of President Yang) and from other veteran units loyal to Deng. Backed by scores of heavy tanks and armored personnel carriers that smashed through the barricades, crushing those who fell in front of them or tried to halt their progress, the troops converged on Tiananmen Square down the wide avenues to its east and west. Armed with automatic weapons, they fired at random on crowds along the streets, at anyone who moved in nearby buildings, and at those who approached too close to their positions.

In the small hours of June 4, troops blocked off all the approaches to Tiananmen Square, and turned off all the lights there. After protracted and anguished debates, the remaining students and demonstrators decided to leave. As they walked out in bedraggled but orderly formation, troops and tanks overran their encampments and crushed the liberty statue to pieces. There followed a period of macabre and terrifying chaos in Peking, as the army gunned down students and citizens both near the square and in other areas of the city. Screams echoed through the night, and flames rose from piles of debris and from army trucks or tanks hit by homemade bombs. Hospitals were overwhelmed by the numbers of dead and wounded, but in many cases were forbidden to treat the civilian casualties. PLA soldiers also died, some killed in terrible ways by enraged crowds who had just seen unarmed demonstrators mowed down. Rumors spread swiftly that the fires in Tiananmen Square were piles of corpses burned by the army to hide the evidence of their cruelty. Whether that was true or not—and no one could get past the troops to check—there were enough bodies in full view elsewhere, lying in the roads, in hospitals, or tangled up in their bicycles where they had fallen, to indicate the scale of the violence. Many hundreds were dead and thousands more wounded. The callousness and randomness of the killings evoked memories of the worst episodes of China's earlier civil wars and the Cultural Revolution. Similar violence was meted out to civilian demonstrators by the armed police in Chengdu and perhaps other cities, but the thoroughness of the government's news blackout made it hard to gauge the scale. Foreign journalists were forbidden to take photographs or conduct interviews, and satellite links abroad were cut.

For a few days rumors swirled that other units of the PLA, shocked by the massacre, might attack the Twenty-seventh Army and start a civil war, or that China's workers would unite in a general strike, or that sympathy riots in other major cities would bring down the government, but none of those things happened. The hard-liners had "won," if that was the right word. Zhao Ziyang was dismissed, the second of Deng's hand-picked "successors" to meet that fate. Li Peng and Deng Xiaoping, in the presence of the most influential party elders—all dressed once again in the traditional high-collared "Mao suits" that were meant to represent a revolutionary simplicity of life-style—publicly thanked the PLA officers and soldiers for clearing the square, and praised their courage. The tough, adept first party secretary of Shanghai, Jiang Zemin, who had maintained order there in the face of massive street demonstrations, was promoted to head the party in Zhao's stead. The party launched a concerted campaign in press, radio, and television blaming the demonstrations on counterrevolutionaries and " hooligans," and mounted an extensive hunt for the student leaders and their main supporters. Many of the "most wanted" students eluded the police for weeks, and several managed to leave China secretly, suggesting the range of public support for their actions and the efficiency and solidarity of their organizations. But thousands of other students were arrested and interrogated. The government also determined to avoid the formation of any autonomous unions of workers, and showed special ferocity toward workers who had joined in the protests. Many were arrested and executed, with maximum publicity.

THE HISTORY OF NATIONS
Chapter 4

China in the Twenty-First Century

Evaluating the Chinese Communist Revolution

By Maurice Meisner

In the following selection, written on the fiftieth anniversary of the Communist revolution, Maurice Meisner reviews the revolution's achievements and failures. Its accomplishments include the establishment of a central government in a country that had been in chaos for over a century, land reform, industrialization, and a dramatic increase in the standard of living. The lack of political reform remains the revolution's major shortcoming. Meisner concludes that despite Mao's intention to create a social utopia, China is essentially a capitalist country. Meisner is Harvey Goldberg Professor of History Emeritus at the University of Wisconsin, Madison, visiting centennial professor at the London School of Economics, and the author of The Deng Xiaoping Era: An Inquiry into the Fate of Chinese Socialism *(1996) and* Mao's China and After *(1999).*

It is easy enough today, after a half-century of the Chinese Communist Party in power, to forget that the "long revolution" that produced the People's Republic of China in 1949 was probably the most popular and certainly the most massive revolution in world history. Those who actively participated in and supported the rural-based Maoist-revolution in the 1930s and 1940s did so in numbers unprecedented in the history of revolutionary movements.

The Chinese Communist revolution was also perhaps the most heroic of all revolutions, a heroism symbolized by the leg-

Maurice Meisner, "China's Communist Revolution: A Half-Century Perspective," *Current History*, vol. 98, September 1999, pp. 243–48. Copyright © 1999 by *Current History*. Reproduced by permission.

endary Long March of the mid-1930s [in which the Communists were forced by nationalist leader Chiang Kai-shek to march more than 6,000 miles into northern China]. But courageous acts were by no means confined to those who embarked on that extraordinary journey, for the revolution's success required enormous sacrifices by tens of millions of people in both cities and villages. The Communist revolution in China was not a coup d'état carried out by a small group of revolutionary conspirators.

Yet revolutions, in the end, are judged not by the numbers who participated or the degree of their heroism, however fascinating and significant these aspects of the original revolutionary act may have been. Rather, revolutions are historically judged and characterized by their ultimate social and political results. What then are the social results of the Maoist revolution that culminated in the political victory of 1949?...

While Maoist ideology and intentions were often ambiguous, the policies of the Communist regime during the early years of the People's Republic were concrete and the accomplishments quite remarkable. The first, and essential, achievement was the fulfillment of the goals of the ill-fated Kuomintang [nationalist party]–Communist alliance of the mid-1920s. The alliance had been forged to pursue two essential nationalist aims: first, national unity (elimination of warlordism and establishment of an effective central government), and, second, national independence (elimination of the foreign encroachments that had humbled and humiliated China for almost a century). But the Kuomintang-Communist alliance floundered in 1927 because of the popular social radicalism it had unleashed, and the victorious Kuomintang regime of Chiang Kai-shek proved ineffective in pursuing its nationalist mission in the years that followed. Yet these elemental nationalist goals of unity and independence, which had proved elusive for so many decades, were achieved by the Communists in a few months following their victory in 1949.

The establishment of an effective central government was an enormous achievement for a country that for more than a century had suffered from internal political disintegration and external impingement, and all the human suffering these entailed. Moreover, the political achievement was the essential prerequisite for progress in all other areas of social and economic life. Among these, in the early years of the new regime were the revival and reformation of China's vice-ridden cities, fundamental

The Long March

sanitation and health measures, the Marriage Law of 1950 (which proclaimed at least formal legal equality between men and women), and the Land Reform campaign of 1950–1952.

Land Reform and Industrialization

Land reform was an especially important accomplishment. It eliminated China's gentry-landlords, the oldest ruling class in world history and a major impediment to modernization. It brought some measure of socioeconomic equity to the Chinese countryside and cemented the powerful tie between the Chinese Communist Party and the majority of peasants. It joined even the most remote villages to a national political structure by implanting party organizations of young peasant activists in localities throughout the countryside. Furthermore, land reform was the essential precondition for modern industrial development. By removing a parasitic landlord class and by establishing an effective political mechanism to channel the agrarian surplus to finance urban industry, the Communist revolution opened the way for the industrial revolution that transformed China from a predominantly agrarian to a mainly industrial nation within a period of several decades. The relationship between land reform and industrialization was understood by Chinese Communist leaders well before Western modernization theorists came across the insight. . . .

Modern industrial development duly began in intensive fashion with the Soviet-modeled first five year plan in 1953. What followed over the remainder of the Mao era (to 1976) and, in even more impressive fashion during the era of Deng Xiaoping (1978–1997), undoubtedly will be recorded as the most rapid process of industrialization over a sustained period in history. For nearly half a century, China, long known as "the sick man of Asia" and among the most impoverished lands by any measurement, has experienced an industrial growth rate averaging 10 percent annually. This has resulted in China's emergence today as the world's second-largest industrial producer (after the United States) and as the country with the third-largest GDP [Gross Domestic Product] (after the United States and Japan) as measured in purchasing power parity.

China's transformation from an agrarian to a primarily industrial nation (in terms of the value of production and probably employment as well) cannot be attributed solely to Deng's market reforms, as is often supposed. The process began under the long rule of Mao, about whose accomplishments many Western scholars have grown strangely silent, fearful that they will be seen as apologists for the crimes of the era should they mention its real accomplishments. Nonetheless, during the Mao period the basic foundations of China's industrial revolution were laid. Without that foundation, the post-Mao reformers would have had little to reform. As distinguished Australian economist Y. Y. Kueh has observed, Maoist China's "sharp rise [30 percent] in industry's share in national income is a rare historical phenomenon. For example, during the first four or five decades of their drive to modern industrialization, the industrial share rose by only 11% in Britain (1801–1841); and 22% in Japan (1882–1927). In the post-war experience of newly industrializing countries, probably only Taiwan has demonstrated as impressive a record as China in this respect."

The social, human, and environmental costs of industrialization have been (and remain) high in China, as has been the case with virtually every industrializing country since the early nineteenth century. In China these costs were paid primarily by the peasantry, the most numerous and poorest members of the population. Yet it is difficult to imagine that there might have been a viable alternative. As sociologist Barrington Moore observed in *Social Origins of Dictatorship and Democracy*, "The tragic fact of the matter is that the poor bear the heaviest costs of modernization under both socialist and capitalist auspices. The only justification for imposing the costs is that they would become steadily worse off without it."

Successes and Failures

During the Mao era the Chinese people as a whole became markedly better-off, even taking into account all the crimes and blunders of the time, among which the famine resulting from the ill-fated Great Leap Forward [an attempt to accelerate economic growth without additional resources] was the most horrendous, claiming an estimated 20 million lives. While the Mao regime certainly exploited the people it ruled, and especially the rural people who put it in power in the first place, the Communist state was not the sole beneficiary of industrialization. During the Mao era significant improvements were made in diet, welfare, health care, and education (especially at the primary level), resulting in a dramatic near-doubling of average life expectancy— from 35 years in pre-1949 China to 65 years in 1976. Moreover, the collectivistic social achievements under Mao greatly facilitated the spectacular economic gains of the market reform era that followed. As Amartya Sen, the Nobel Prize–winning Cambridge economist, has forcefully argued, the extensive development of public education, health care, and social security during the Mao era (in contrast to India's meager accomplishments in these areas) was crucial in promoting and sustaining economic growth in the Deng era. . . .

The great failure of Maoism was not economic but political. Not only did the Maoist regime fail to realize the democratic hopes aroused by the revolution, it also failed to fulfill its socialist promises. Mao's China was not socialist. It lacked, in both conception and reality, the essential feature of a socialist society, traditionally conceived as a system whereby the immediate producers control the conditions and products of their labor. Nor was there any conception, much less the reality, of the democratic political form that such a socialist society necessarily would assume, what Marx termed "the self-government of the producers."

Thus it was not the case, as charged by some and celebrated by others, that Deng Xiaoping's market reforms dismantled the socialism of the Mao era. In truth, there was no socialist system to destroy. Historical accuracy is ill-served by the conventional image of Mao as an ideological fanatic who sacrificed modern economic development to an all-consuming quest for a socialist spiritual utopia. Precisely the opposite would be closer to the historical record. It was more often the case that socialist goals and values were sacrificed to the imperatives of economic development.

While the Maoist economic record was impressive in its time, that time had passed by the early 1970s. Maoism had exhausted its once great creative energies and was no longer capable of providing inspiration to an increasingly disillusioned population. The modern industrial plant, now large, was also cumbersome and increasingly inefficient, requiring ever-larger infusions of capital to maintain high rates of growth. The Maoist method of financing industrialization—essentially state exploitation of the villages—could not have continued long without pauperizing the peasantry, the social base of the Communist revolution and the Maoist regime. But a dogmatized Maoism was no longer capable of new initiatives. It fell to Deng Xiaoping to bring about the necessary fundamental changes for the survival of the regime and the preservation of the material gains of the revolution.

Deng Xiaoping's Contribution

When Deng and his reformist colleagues inaugurated their program of market restructuring in 1979, it was not their intention to create a capitalist economy. "Socialist democracy" was Deng's promise, a slogan that appealed to an urban population increasingly conscious that Maoist China lacked genuine socialism as well as democracy. There is no reason to question the sincerity of the reformers' promise. Deng and his supporters believed that capitalist techniques could be borrowed selectively to quicken the pace and improve the quality of China's economic development. This (they assumed in orthodox Marxist fashion) would establish the proper material base for the construction of a socialist society in the future. Much in the fashion of China's late-nineteenth-century conservative modernizers, it was assumed that capitalism was not necessarily an organic whole—and that its material accomplishments could be neatly separated from bourgeois society and culture. An eventual socialist outcome would be guaranteed, Deng believed, by maintaining state control over the "commanding heights" of the economy and especially by preserving the political primacy of the Chinese Communist Party, whose leaders presumably held the socialist goal steadfastly in mind. "Political power is firmly in our hands," Deng once reassured those who were skeptical that his economic policies would have a socialist outcome.

The economic results of the post-Mao market reforms have been spectacular. The seemingly utopian goal of quadrupling the size of the Chinese economy by the year 2000, announced at the beginning of the reform period, was in fact achieved by 1995. And some observers now predict that China will overtake the United States as the world's largest economy by the year 2015.

The social results have been less salutary: growing and glaring socioeconomic inequalities, the emergence of new class divisions in both towns and villages, an orgy of official profiteering and bureaucratic corruption, the partial collapse of the social welfare system, the deterioration of public health care and education, new forms of sexual inequality, and accelerated environmental destruction.

These and the other unintended social consequences of post-Maoist economic policies are well known both to foreign observers and the Chinese government, even if the efforts on the part of the latter to alleviate the maladies thus far have been feeble. What must be stressed is that the most general and historically far-reaching result of market reform has been the construction of a capitalist economy that now functions in accordance with its own dynamics. The phenomenon deserves emphasis since the use of the term capitalism to describe the contemporary Chinese order is well beyond the pale of acceptable official discourse in China today because it obviously clashes with Beijing's need to claim a socialist legitimacy. Most foreign scholars of contemporary Chinese affairs also seem reluctant to use the term, for reasons that are less clear.

China as Capitalist

Nonetheless, what has emerged from Deng's reforms—and this has been especially clear since the early 1990s—is an essentially capitalist economy. First, it is a system based largely on wage labor (which was also partially the case during the Mao era but is now overwhelmingly dominant). Second, China has been integrated into the world capitalist economy through Deng's "open door" policies—and this has been a powerful force for molding the domestic economy in accordance with global capitalist norms. Third, the eminently capitalist principle of profit making has been universalized as the main precept in the functioning of enterprises and the conduct of economic life in general. Fourth, labor has been fully commodified with the success of the long and agonizing campaign to "smash the iron rice bowl" in urban state factories and the abolition of the rural communes. The latter, it might be noted, yielded a surplus labor population numbering some 200 million, many of whom became low-paid wage laborers in the burgeoning rural industrial sector (the township and village enterprises). Others were thrown into the ranks of China's massive "floating population," the migrant laborers who wander from city to city seeking such temporary work as they can find.

Fifth, to ensure the construction and proper operation of a market economy, the Communist state promoted entrepreneurship, in effect breeding a new bourgeoisie, the essential social agent of capitalist development. In addition, the process of creating a market economy was ideologically facilitated by the propagation of new values, especially those promoting individual acquisitiveness ("to get rich is glorious") and sanctioning inequality ("some must get rich first").

With the maturation of these policies in the early 1990s, especially the creation of a new bourgeoisie (albeit one with a strong bureaucratic component) and a labor market, China has had a flourishing capitalist market economy that functions largely within the norms that govern capitalism in general. Chinese capitalism is clearly not yet entirely developed, most notably lacking a full-fledged system of private property. Nonetheless, virtually all economic enterprises, whatever their formal ownership status, function as capitalist entities in a land that is undergoing the most massive and perhaps the most rapid process of capitalist development and proletarianization in history.

Damming the Yangtze River to Meet China's Energy Needs

By Sandra Burton

Energy production and environmental protection are two major issues facing China in the twenty-first century. Much of China's energy is currently produced by coal-burning power plants that cause serious air pollution. The Chinese hope that the hydroelectric power produced by damming the Yangtze (Chang Jiang) River will reduce some of that air pollution. To this end, they have begun construction of the Three Gorges Dam, which is slated for completion by 2015. Here Sandra Burton reviews pros and cons of the project. Although it will reduce pollution, critics say that the dam will cause environmental problems—such as upstream flooding and silt buildups that will hamper river navigation—as well as major population displacements. Sandra Burton is the Hong Kong bureau chief for Time.

The world's largest dam is under way in China, but it won't solve the country's giant energy problems. Midway between its icy source in Tibet and the fertile delta at its mouth in Shanghai, 3,900 miles to the east, China's Yangtze River hurtles through a series of sheer chasms known as the Three Gorges. Legend has it that the scenic channel was carved in stone by the goddess Yao Ji as a way of diverting the river around the petrified remains of a dozen dragons she had slain for harassing the peasants. Over the centuries painters and poets have idealized the canyons as a mist-shrouded wilderness. While that may have once been true, the region lost much of its majesty in

Sandra Burton, "Taming the River Wild," *Time*, vol. 144, December 19, 1994, p. 62. Copyright © 1994 by Time, Inc. Reproduced by permission.

modern times, as demolition teams blasted rocky obstructions from the river's course, and the bucolic villages on its banks gave way to grim new factory towns.

Now both visions of the Three Gorges—the ideal and the real—are about to be consigned to a watery grave. [In December 1994] Chinese Premier Li Peng will preside over the symbolic first pouring of concrete in what is intended to be the world's largest hydroelectric dam. Already, mammoth earthworks on both banks of the construction site have begun to constrict the flow of the river where it gushes forth from the Xiling Gorge. Over the next 14 years, if all goes as planned, first an earthen coffer dam and then a 200-yd.-high concrete spillway and adjacent set of ship-lifting locks will block the swirling channel, transforming the Three Gorges into a single deep and currentless reservoir. Covering everything from ancient temples to contemporary slag heaps,

FREE RIVER, FREE SPEECH

Investigative journalist and environmental activist Dai Qing was jailed for ten months after the 1989 crackdown in Tiananmen Square because of her work Yangtze, Yangtze, *which criticized the construction of the Three Gorges Dam on the Yangtze (Chang Jiang) River. Here she laments the suppression of criticism of the project.*

The Three Gorges Dam Project, the largest hydroelectric power project ever proposed, will, if completed, place on the Yangtzi River the highest dam in the world. It is to be built on the midstream of the main current of the third largest river in the world. The project as planned will take roughly twenty years to complete, and the budget is set at $100 billion. The number of people to be uprooted from their homeland—1.2 million. . . .

Right now, censorship of opposing opinions is even more severe than it has been in the past. No essays can be published in any of the important domestic newspapers and magazines within China. There is still no way to organize any kind of debate about the project. . . .

Emily Merino

the water will flood 28,000 acres of farmland and 20 towns and drive 1.4 million people from their homes.

The gigantic Three Gorges project has inspired awe and opposition ever since it was first proposed 75 years ago by modern China's founding father, Sun Yat-sen. During the 1980s the dam plan became a favorite target of pro-democracy dissidents. It was not until 1992, three years after the critics were brutally silenced in Tiananmen Square, that the communist rulers rammed the project through the National People's Congress. Even today, as construction finally gets rolling, the dam still draws fire from environmentalists around the world. To opponents, it is a symbol of mankind's monstrous interventions in nature, an enterprise that will not only displace people but also devastate wildlife and alter the landscape forever. . . .

Chinese leaders argue just as vehemently that Three Gorges is

---

If the dam is such a fantastic idea, a unique feat of engineering, as is claimed, then why in Heaven's name is the government unwilling to allow a public debate on the subject in China? If not a public debate, then why can't scientists and specialists discuss the pros and cons of the project? A number of journalists including myself managed to edit and publish a volume of dissenting opinion regarding the dam before the authorities pushed through the decision to go ahead with the project in 1989. After the suppression of June 4, the government ordered the book pulped and banned from re-publication. That ban remains in force to this day. What was our crime? They say we had "contributed to creating the atmosphere of public opinion that led to the turmoil and riots" of 1989! . . .

An ancient Chinese philosopher said this: it is even more dangerous to silence the people than to dam a river. Four thousand years on and the message to our present rulers remains the same: let the people speak out; let the river run free.

Dai Qing, "Three River Gorges Dam Project and Free Speech in China," *Chicago Review*, 1993, vol. 39, issue 3/4, p. 275.

vital to their country's future—and actually good for the environment as a whole. They say it will prevent the periodic flooding that has claimed 500,000 lives in this century. More important, its production of clean hydroelectric power will reduce China's reliance on coal, the dirtiest of all fossil fuels, which now supplies 75% of the country's energy needs. The burning of coal has cast a pall of pollution over major Chinese cities and helped make pulmonary disease the nation's leading cause of death.

The issue is how a rapidly growing nation of 1.2 billion people, all of whom would like refrigerators and other conveniences, can promote economic development without wrecking its environment. For the Chinese government, hydropower in general and Three Gorges in particular are a big part of the solution. "The advantages outweigh the disadvantages," contends He Gong, vice president of the China Yangtze Three Gorges Project Development Corp.

How China meets its energy needs has an impact far beyond its boundaries. Sulfurous emissions from Chinese power plants and factories blow eastward and fall as acid rain on Japan and Korea. In fact, the pollution has planet-wide implications: China is the world's second-largest producer of carbon dioxide and other greenhouse gases that are collecting in the atmosphere and may, many scientists believe, lead to global warming. If China maintains its annual economic growth rate of 11%, the country will need to add 17,000 megawatts of electrical generating capacity each year for the rest of the [1990s]. Within 10 years, that would be as much new power as the U.S. generates overall today. If China uses mostly coal to produce that power, the greenhouse effect could be catastrophic.

Many opponents of Three Gorges have no quarrel with the effort to move away from coal toward hydropower. But they argue that for a lower price, numerous smaller dams could produce more power and greater flood-control benefits. They fear that a dam so large on the notoriously muddy Yangtze will lead to dangerous buildups of silt in some parts of the river, creating new obstacles to navigation and causing floods upstream. Chinese officials respond that both big and small dams are needed. Indeed, 10 projects smaller than Three Gorges, with a total capacity of nearly 12,000 megawatts, are under construction on the upper reaches of the Yangtze and its tributaries.

Whether or not Three Gorges is ever finished, hydropower

can never meet the bulk of China's energy needs. Part of the problem is that most of the potential dam sites are in the less populated southwestern part of the country, making it expensive to transmit electricity to the industrial north and east. Experts say hydropower will account for no more than 20% of China's electricity generation by 2010.

Nuclear plants are another clean power source, at least in terms of air pollution, but splitting the atom won't solve China's energy problems either. The government's controls on electricity prices and its failure to adopt international nuclear-safety standards have discouraged foreign investors from helping China build commercial reactors. Only two nuclear plants are in operation, and one of those was built to supply electricity mainly to Hong Kong at rates five times as high as what can be charged in China. Jiang Xinxiong, president of the China Nuclear Industry Corp., predicts that 20 more atom plants will be on line by 2020, but even so, nuclear power would meet less than 10% of China's energy needs.

That leaves no way around a heavy dependence on coal. The best China can hope for, say experts, is to cut coal's portion of the energy mix from 75% to 60% by 2010. The imperative, then, is to find cleaner, more efficient ways to burn the plentiful fossil fuel, reducing emissions of carbon dioxide, sulfur compounds and the incompletely combusted particles that form soot. . . .

Even if coal is burned cleanly and efficiently, it produces large amounts of carbon dioxide, the most common greenhouse gas. To help ease the threat of global warming, China might use new technology to convert a portion of its coal reserves to natural gas, which delivers much more energy for the amount of CO_2 released. The process, though, is expensive. . . .

While foreigners may be justifiably reluctant to help finance a project as audacious and controversial as Three Gorges, many indisputably worthy ventures, from coal gasification to experiments with solar power, are also begging for funds. Governments and investors naturally wonder if they can afford to gamble on China. But as the most populous nation threatens to pollute the entire planet, can the rest of the world afford to turn its back?

The Conflict over Tibet

By Orville Schell

Tibet has always had an uneasy relationship with the Han Chinese, dating back to A.D. 763, when the Tibetans attacked and looted Chang'an (Xi'an), the Tang dynasty capitol. Tibet was a vassal state under the Qing dynasty in the early twentieth century, was considered part of China by the Nationalist Kumintang, and is still considered Chinese territory by the current Communist government. No country has ever recognized Tibet as an independent nation.

Tibet was traditionally a feudal region where 95 percent of the population were serfs or slaves owned by nobles or monasteries. The People's Liberation Army (PLA) invaded Tibet in 1950 to reunite all parts of China and to liberate the Tibetans from feudalism. The Tibetans did not want to be liberated by the PLA. Thousands were killed in the invasion and in an uprising in 1959. Thousands more fled to India when the uprising was suppressed. Among the refugees was the Dalai Lama, the spiritual leader of Tibet. Many more Tibetans died in the famine of 1960–1961. Demonstrations and violence broke out again in the 1980s and were suppressed by the Chinese government.

In this selection from his book Virtual Tibet, *Orville Schell reviews the Tibetan-Chinese relationship of the past fifty years. Schell says that the Han Chinese see themselves as bringing Tibet into the modern world and developing the region economically. Many Tibetans, on the other hand, believe they have been robbed of their culture and autonomy. The situation is complicated, Schell says, by the Western movement for Tibetan "liberation" from the Chinese. While Tibetans and their Western supporters advocate for Tibetan autonomy, the Chinese government retains control of the area. Schell is dean of the Graduate School of Journalism, University of California at Berkeley, and author of many works on China, including* Mandate of Heaven *and* The China Reader.

When Kublai Khan conquered China and set up the Mongol Yuan dynasty in Beijing in 1279, Tibet became a peripheral part of this new empire, wedded to China, in a manner of speaking, by a "barbarian" matchmaker. Under the Ming dynasty (1368–1642), Tibet's relations with China continued, although in a considerably diminished manner. While Chinese emperors conferred honorific titles on certain Tibetan notables, they exerted none of the political authority that the Mongols had enjoyed. In 1662, however, when another "barbarian" tribe, the Manchus, overthrew the Ming to set up the Qing dynasty, they began to jockey for power over Tibet. A complicated series of shifting alliances between the Tibetans, the Mongols, and the Manchus finally brought Qing troops, allied with the seventh Dalai Lama, to Lhasa itself in 1720; and in 1721, in a decree issued in the name of the Qing court, Tibet was declared a vassal state. To consolidate their protectorate, the Manchus henceforth posted a military garrison and a handful of imperial representatives, or *ambans*, in Lhasa.

Until the twentieth century, the West was little more than a footnote in Tibetan history. An irony of Tibet's current relations with the West is that for two centuries its celebrated resistance to Western intrusion, its very "forbiddenness," was as much imposed by a wary and conservative Tibetan clergy as by suspicious Chinese *ambans* who did not want to see that land become a back door into China for European imperialists.

In 1904, the worst fears of both came to pass when Colonel Francis Younghusband's expeditionary force set off from India for Lhasa. Worried that czarist Russia had designs on this remote region, the British viceroy in India dispatched Younghusband with just over a thousand British and Indian troops to force the Tibetans to renounce any intention of allying with Saint Petersburg. The expedition would ultimately march all the way to the "forbidden city" and leave a toll of several thousand dead and wounded Tibetans behind.

In the wake of this incursion, the ailing Qing dynasty sent an army of its own to Lhasa to reassert its administrative and military authority. But time had run out on China's last imperial dynasty. In 1911, the Qing was overthrown, its troops were expelled from Lhasa, and Tibet entered a period of almost forty years during which it exercised virtual independence over its affairs.

De Facto Independence

During these decades, Tibet achieved many of the hallmarks of self-rule: a functioning government, a tax system, its own currency, a postal system, and a small military. The Tibetans even negotiated certain agreements directly with the British as if they were a sovereign power. "Whatever political theorists might say," Hugh E. Richardson, former head of the British mission in Lhasa, would write in his 1962 book, *Tibet and Its History*, "the Tibetan government could and did follow a course of action completely independent of the government of China." Indeed, even the representative of Chiang Kai-shek's Nationalist government, Shen Tsung-lien, who arrived in Lhasa in 1946, acknowledged in his own book, *Tibet and the Tibetans*, that the country had enjoyed de facto independence since 1911.

Yet Tibet was not quite a nation in the European sense. Indeed, at no time did any Western power come out in favor of its independence or grant it diplomatic recognition, and in the minds of the Chinese Nationalists and Communists alike, Tibet, like Taiwan, continued to be viewed as a de jure and integral part of China.

Mao's Attempts to Reunify China

After the Communist Party's victory over Chiang's Nationalists in 1949, Mao Zedong set about reunifying all the errant pieces of China's old multiethnic empire, traditionally viewed as including *han* (Central Chinese), *man* (Manchus), *meng* (Mongolians), *hui* (Moslems), and *zang* (Tibetans). Indeed, as it had been for the founders of so many previous Chinese dynasties, the task of reunification was viewed by Mao's revolutionary government as an almost sacred obligation. Since it was the official Party view that China had been "dismembered"—literally *fen'gua,* or "cut up like a melon"—by predatory imperialist powers, reunification was a tangible way for Mao to show the world that China had, in fact, finally "stood up" and would henceforth strive aggressively to restore and defend its sovereignty and territorial integrity.

Officials in Lhasa responded with alarm to China's declarations that it wished to "liberate" Tibet from feudal bondage. They tried to beef up their backward military and break out of their self-imposed isolation. In October 1950, however, after negotiations failed, the People's Liberation Army (PLA) began a military occupation of Eastern Tibet, and soon thereafter the Dalai Lama fled Lhasa with his cabinet for the Indian border. In the spring of 1951, after the United Nations refused to consider Tibet's appeals for help, a Tibetan delegation finally went to Beijing and signed an accord, the Seventeen-Point Agreement for the Peaceful Liberation of Tibet, but without the Dalai Lama's approval. The agreement acknowledged Chinese sovereignty—"The Tibetan people shall return to the big family of the motherland"—in return for a promise of "national regional autonomy" that would allow Tibetans to maintain their traditional religious, political, and economic systems until "the people raise demands for reform." But it also granted China the right to set up a military headquarters in Lhasa.

After the Dalai Lama's return to Lhasa, for a while a fragile peace looked like it might hold. Indeed, it is often forgotten now that in the early 1950s the Dalai Lama himself was quite sympathetic to some of the liberationist sentiments then sweeping Mao's China. In a conversation several years ago, he told me that, threatening as he found the Chinese, the Communist Party's emphasis on serving the oppressed and championing the commonweal over the interests of private individuals appealed to him. . . .

The Chinese Communists, of course, viewed old Tibet through their own ideological lenses as a decadent and oppressive society in which ordinary people had been exploited by serfdom, theocratic rule, and a land-tenure system stacked in favor of the aristocracy and the clergy. Indeed, there were many aspects of Tibet's feudal social and political system that were deeply unjust and autocratic. What held the fabric of Tibetan life together, however, was the common bond of Buddhism, which gave at least the illusion of a shared purpose and meaning to every level of society. But where this belief system might have seemed to a nomad or serf a sacred and unalterable fact of life, to Communists steeped in the notion of religion as the opium of the masses, it was anathema. They viewed Tibet's traditional society, where the vast majority of the population were illiterate and many were virtually "owned" by noble landholding families or monasteries, as feudal in the extreme. As Marshal Chen Yi described it on a visit to Lhasa, China's ultimate commitment was to "rid Tibet of its backward situation."

When China began dismantling monasteries, forcing the organization of agricultural cooperatives, and initiating "democratic reforms" in Kham, or Eastern Tibet, conflict quickly arose. By

1956, opposition had catalyzed into armed resistance. It was at this time that the American Central Intelligence Agency began aiding Tibetan guerrillas, even transporting several hundred of them to Camp Hale in Colorado for military training.

The fighting culminated in 1959 with an uprising in Lhasa against the Chinese occupation. In March of that year, the Dalai Lama fled once again, this time all the way to Dharamsala, India, where he set up a government in exile. He would sadly remember departing Lhasa "in a daze of sickness and weariness and unhappiness deeper than I can express."

When the Cultural Revolution swept through Tibet in the mid-1960s, Red Guards, not a few of whom were themselves young Tibetans, launched a form of class warfare, savagely attacking what the Party described as all "remnants of old customs, values, and beliefs." Before the political paroxysm was spent, almost all Tibet's monasteries were in ruins, thousands of monks had been imprisoned or murdered, almost every aristocrat had had his property expropriated, and ordinary people had had their religious lives radically circumscribed. Animosity between Tibetans and Han Chinese rose to dangerous levels.

A Few Years of Hope

After Mao's death in 1976, the relatively liberal Hu Yaobang became Party general secretary and Beijing's policy toward Tibet softened considerably. Returning from a 1980 trip to Tibet that evidently shocked him, Hu called on all Party cadres to implement new "flexible policies suited to conditions in Tibet," including more autonomy and support for indigenous Tibetan culture, albeit still "under the unified leadership of the party Central Committee." Negotiations with representatives of the Dalai Lama were then initiated and several fact-finding missions composed of supporters of the government in exile were allowed to visit Tibet.

What finally ended these few years of hopeful moderation when reconciliation might have been possible was a spate of anti-Chinese riots in support of Tibetan independence that broke out in Lhasa in September 1987. By the end of October, a number of Tibetan monks had been shot by the police and Lhasa was again seething with tension. When in March 1988 and again in 1989 anti-Chinese proindependence demonstrators once again took to the streets of the city, Beijing declared martial law. The crackdown represented a stark end to Beijing's willingness to resolve the Tibet question through compromise. These disturbances and Beijing's ongoing militant insistence that Tibet was a sovereign part of China set off a global debate over the rights of an ethnically distinct, linguistically different, culturally unique, geographically separate people who had attained a high level of de facto self-rule to gain self-determination from the sovereign claims of a multiethnic state like the People's Republic of China.

Needless to say, each side of this unequal standoff had an elaborate and carefully, if selectively, researched version of history that supported its own claims. That both versions have a certain polemical coherence and a certain quotient of truth only makes sorting out the intricacies of his fractious relationship all the more daunting.

Western and Chinese Views of Tibet

During these years of upheaval, the Tibetan government in exile adopted an aggressive new strategy for gaining support for their cause: a global publicity campaign to portray Tibetans as the victims of Chinese oppression. Instead of simply seeking to win concessions through negotiations, they also began vigorously to court world opinion through organizations like the International Campaign for Tibet, an advocacy group based in Washington, D.C., and through more frequent high-visibility trips abroad by the Dalai Lama. Unfortunately, the effort succeeded in antagonizing China even as it ignited new support for a Tibet already on the figurative hard drives of many Westerners. And so, a whole new chapter in the history of the West's vicarious involvement with that land began. Western respect for and fascination with the Dalai Lama took a quantum leap in 1989 when he was awarded the Nobel Peace Prize. But it was a grand humiliation for China to have its first Nobel Peace Prize winner be a minority dissident in exile, and Sino-Tibetan relations entered an even more intractable phase.

Often forgotten in this controversy was the fact that by 1994 China had invested over $4 billion in Tibet and had initiated over sixty major new infrastructure projects there. In 1996 alone, Beijing pumped another $600 million into this essentially nonproductive protectorate. The rights and wrongs of the situation aside, many were left wondering whether Tibet could realistically hope to make it alone, should independence ever be offered.

As of today, Beijing's position remains more rigid than ever, even as the posture of the Dalai Lama has become considerably more flexible, especially on the question of independence. In 1988, he suggested that Tibet be granted not outright independence but some kind of political autonomy "founded on a constitution of basic law" and a form of government that would give Tibet "the right to decide on all affairs relating to Tibet and Tibetans," while leaving matters of defense and foreign affairs in the hands of Beijing.

China, however, has shown few signs of reappraising its hardline approach. Indeed, even President Clinton's unusual exchange with [PRC] President Jiang Zenin of China during a June 1998 summit in Beijing did little to thaw the situation. "I have spent time with the Dalai Lama," Clinton cheerfully quipped to Jiang. "I believe him to be an honest man, and I believe if he had a conversation with President Jaing, they would like each other very much." Two years later, China's posture toward Tibet was as uncompromising as ever. Raidi (some Tibetans use a single name), the chairman of the People's Congress of Tibet, and Legqog, the head of the Beijing-appointed Tibetan Autonomous Region government, were blaming the United States, Britain, and the Dharamsala government for its support of Tibetan separatists and vilifying the Dalai Lama as "the chief representative of the feudal serf system" that had reduced the Tibetan people to "animal status." Of course, Jiang like other Chinese, tends not to romanticize Tibet as many Westerners do. Indeed, he expressed incredulity that those who live in countries where "education in science and technology has developed to a very high level" and where "people are now enjoying modern civilization" should still "have a belief in Lamaism."

Many observers believe that Beijing has simply decided to wait until the sixty-five-year-old (as of July 6, 2000) Dalai Lama passes from the scene and is counting on Tibet to become ever more Sinicized and so more amenable to Chinese rule. (The area currently included in the so-called Tibetan Autonomous Region contains fewer than half the ethnic Tibetans in China. And due to the massive PLA presence and the recent wave of government-sanctioned immigration from the border regions of Qinghai, Gansu, Sichuan, and Yunnan provinces, the Tibetan Autonomous Region now has almost as many Han Chinese as Tibetans.)

The Uighur Independence Movement

By Nader Hasan

The Uighur minority group in China's far northwest has a different language, culture, and history than the Han Chinese, and they identify with other Islamic peoples in Asia. In the following selection, Nader Hasan, the senior editor of the Harvard International Review, *describes the Uighur movement for autonomy. As the Uighurs chafe under Han Chinese rule, militant separatists have committed terrorist acts, especially bombings, in both their homeland of Xinjiang and elsewhere in China. The Chinese have brutally suppressed the Uighur nationalistic movement. In recent years, Beijing has attempted to connect Uighur separatists to international Islamic extremists and terrorists, including Afghanistan's Taliban.*

While the struggles for liberation in Kosovo, East Timor, and Chechnya have taken turns capturing the world's attention, the Chinese province of Xinjiang is quietly continuing its own rebellion. This predominantly Muslim region has been chafing under Chinese authority for over 400 years, and it shows no signs of stopping. Sharing neither religion, language, nor ethnicity with the country's majority Han Chinese, the Uighurs of Xinjiang province are eager to assert their nationhood. Anti-government activity since the fall of the Soviet Union has been on the rise. Clashes between protesters and Chinese authorities are becoming increasingly violent and frequent, and executions for "counter-revolutionary activity" have become almost weekly occurrences, increasing foreign awareness of the human rights violations in the region.

While the West prefers to bestow its sympathies upon neighboring Tibet, the international media has begun to open its eyes to the oppression of the Uighurs. China appears to have adopted a two-pronged approach to quell dissent; while quickly executing suspected Uighur nationalists, Beijing has also encouraged mass immigration of Han Chinese to the region to dilute the preponderance of the majority Uighur population. These tactics have brought mixed success. While Xinjiang remains under Chinese control, the Uighurs have grown increasingly resentful toward the government and the immigrant Han.

Known today as the Xinjiang Uighur Autonomous Region, China's largest province has long played a major role in the geopolitics of Central Asia. Its location in the northwestern corner of China, stretching from the Gobi Desert to the Himalayas, made it the historic meeting place of ancient Chinese, Persian, and Turkic empires. As a result, it has fallen under the yoke of many different rulers, each of whom affected the ethnic and cultural makeup of the region. . . .

It was not until the early 1700s, under the Manchu Qing dynasty, that China reestablished military control of what is now Xinjiang. It remained under Chinese control until the mid-19th century, when, weakened by frequent, albeit unsuccessful rebellions, parts of the region fell under Russian and British control. After enjoying a brief period of independence between 1864 and 1877, Eastern Turkestan (whose borders approximate today's Xinjiang) was retaken by China and declared an official Chinese province in 1884. Frequent rebellions remained unsuccessful until 1944, when the Uighurs took advantage of the turmoil generated by World War II to establish the East Turkestan Republic (ETR). At the time, lasting sovereignty seemed possible, as Mao Zedong had promised autonomy for China's minority groups in an effort to bolster support for his Chinese Communist Party (CCP). However, most of the ETR leadership died in a mysterious plane crash en route to Beijing for negotiations with the CCP. After their victory in the Chinese civil war, Mao's troops moved into Xinjiang and brought the province under communist control. The years that followed were turbulent for the Uighurs. During the Cultural Revolution (1966–1976), mosques were closed, the Qu'ran and other religious texts were burned, religious leaders were arrested, and thousands were sentenced to labor camps.

Spread of Islamic Nationalism

Although the Xinjiang independence movement lay dormant for years under the stern rule of Chairman Mao, Uighur nationalism gained momentum under the more lenient cultural and religious policies of the 1980s. The fall of the Soviet Union gave hope to the Uighurs of Xinjiang, as Islamic nationalist movements emerged across the newly independent states of Central Asia—Uzbekistan, Kazakhstan, Tajikistan, Kyrgyzstan, and Turkmenistan. The long-isolated province suddenly felt the presence of potential allies in the region.

A lapse in border control accompanied the fall of Soviet communism, and arms from the former Soviet states flowed into Xinjiang and the hands of militant separatists. Violent demonstrations and car bombings became the norm in the capital, Urumqi, and in Kashgar, Xinjiang's second-largest city. Xinjiang's governor, Ablait Abdureschit, told reporters in early 1998 that "since the start of the 1990s, if you count explosions, assassinations and other terrorist activities, it comes to a few thousand incidents."

Beijing regards separatism in Xinjiang as a serious threat to China's national security, and is taking measures to curb it. In 1998, the government abruptly fired 260 Uighur officials in the province and halted the construction or renovation of 133 mosques. Teaching of the Qu'ran and other religious texts was once again banned.

Although the crackdown has succeeded in reducing violence, it has not diminished antigovernment sentiment. Unlike Chechnya or even Afghanistan, where rebellion was orchestrated by a few militant leaders, a majority of the Uighur population of Xinjiang supports independence from China. Many Uighurs believe that they do not belong in China, a country whose majority they share neither language, religion, nor heritage with. The Uighurs' unwillingness to submit to Chinese authority and their kinship with the Islamic states of the region make Xinjiang the most serious internal security threat to China in the eyes of the Beijing leadership.

Breaking the Impasse on Human Rights

By Harry Harding

The issue of human rights continues to be a major conflict point in China-U.S. relations. The very notion of "human rights" is viewed differently by the two nations. Harry Harding, dean of the Elliott School of International Affairs and professor of political science and international affairs at George Washington University, describes these differences and makes some specific suggestions on how the human rights issue might be more effectively managed. Harding calls on the Chinese to reform their political system. In addition, he says the United States must expand its current concept of human rights and take a long-term view toward the development of democracy in China. Harding is the author of A Fragile Relationship: The United States and China Since 1972 *and other books.*

Ever since the mid–1980s, and especially since the Tiananmen crisis of 1989, human rights has been one of the most prominent and contentious issues in U.S.-China relations. The U.S. government, many American nongovernmental organizations, and much of the American press have repeatedly criticized the absence of democracy and the violations of human rights in China. The United States has employed a variety of measures—from private diplomacy to public criticism to threats of economic sanctions—to try to force change in China's system of governance and to gain greater respect for human rights in China.

Unfortunately, none of these measures has achieved significant or lasting results. The Chinese government has occasionally made a few gestures to mollify American critics, such as releasing a few dissidents from prison, or promising to allow international inspections of its prisons. In general, however, China's treatment of political dissent, autonomous labor unions, or independent religious organizations has not improved since 1989. Indeed, most human rights organizations in the United States would say that the human rights situation in China has continued to deteriorate.

But examining the same record, many Chinese would come to a different conclusion. They would argue that, despite the Tiananmen crisis, the last two decades have seen marked progress in promoting human rights in their country. The overall political situation has remained stable. The standard of living for the majority of the population has improved, in many cases dramatically. Ordinary people have greater freedom from government or party intervention in their daily lives. There has been widespread progress in enhancing the rule of law, in enlarging the power of legislative bodies, and in popularizing competitive local elections. Chinese find it difficult to understand why American observers fail to acknowledge that these improvements have taken place.

Impasse

Thus China and the U.S. have reached an impasse over human rights. Where Chinese see progress, Americans see stagnation, even retrogression. Where Americans see grounds for criticism, many Chinese find reasons for satisfaction.

This impasse over human rights has undermined the broader Sino-American relationship. The perception that China systematically violates the human rights of its people has greatly exacerbated American concerns about a number of other issues. Many Americans now worry that China will drastically limit the exercise of political freedom in Hong Kong, once it regains sovereignty over that territory. [Hong Kong returned to China in 1997.] Others believe that the absence of democratic institutions in China makes it more likely that China will engage in aggressive or uncooperative international behavior as its economic and military power grows. Still others argue that Beijing's growing trade surplus with the United States is the result of the use of child and prison labor to produce goods for export, as well as the maintenance of artificially low wages through the chronic suppression of independent trade unions.

At the same time, the human rights issue has also significantly damaged Chinese perceptions of the United States. Many Chinese, ordinary people as well as government officials, believe that the American preoccupation with human rights is the latest evidence that the United States remains a hegemonic power, which tries to interfere in the internal affairs of other countries in order to impose its political system and cultural values on them. The purpose of that intervention, many Chinese now believe, is to keep China weak and divided, by undermining the central government, by encouraging regional separatism, and by fomenting social unrest. In this way, American policy toward human rights in China is perceived not only as ill-informed, but also as ill-intentioned.

The impasse over human rights is thus a highly emotional one. It touches some of the core values in each society: the American values of freedom, individualism, and democracy, and the Chinese values of sovereignty, national pride, and self-determination. It evokes each society's core myths: America's missionary responsibility to carry freedom and democracy overseas, and China's struggle against foreign intervention in its internal affairs. Increasingly, too, it is related to the shift in the relative power of the two countries: China's determination to become strong, and America's desire to maintain its leadership role in international affairs. Managing this complex and controversial issue will test the two countries' ability to develop and maintain a stable and cooperative relationship. How can China and the United States avoid chronic tension, let alone acute confrontation, over the issue of human rights? . . .

Managing the Human Rights Issue

Breaking this impasse requires a fresh approach to the human rights dimension in Sino-American relations. This new strategy will not enable the two countries to reach complete consensus on the issue of human rights. But it will permit them to *identify their common interests* on the issue of governance in China, to *develop cooperative programs* for pursuing those common interests, and to *identify appropriate strategies* for addressing their remaining differences. The overall aim of the approach is to transform the human rights issue from confrontation to at least partial cooperation.

A Comprehensive Definition

1. *The United States should adopt a more comprehensive definition of human rights, so as to include social and economic rights as well as political and civil freedoms.*

In recent years, the United States has been preoccupied with the state of individual political and civil freedoms in other countries: freedom of expression, freedom of organization, freedom of protest, freedom of religion, the existence of opposition political parties, free and competitive elections, freedom from torture, the right to legal counsel, and the right to a fair and speedy trial.. . .

The American preoccupation with political and civil liberties has several shortcomings. The U.S. appears indifferent to the concerns of people of poorer countries for subsistence and development. And by focusing on the fate of a relatively small number of political dissidents, the U.S. may give the impression that it is in favor of instability and disorder. Such a narrow definition also minimizes the areas of common interest between the United States and countries like China, and magnifies the areas of disagreement.

Thus the United States should adopt a broader concept of human rights. Specifically, it should pay as much attention to the protection of social and economic rights as to the promotion of political and civil liberties. And in the sphere of political and civil liberties, it is preferable for the U.S. to focus on the promotion of institutional reforms, rather than on the fate of individual dissidents. As important as the release of political prisoners may be to the individuals and their families, it does nothing to reform the political and legal institutions that imprisoned them in the first place. . . . .

Longer-Term Perspective

2. *The United States should adopt a longer-term perspective toward the issue of democratization.*

Most Americans naturally equate the promotion of human rights with the promotion of democracy. Ultimately, they believe, the establishment and protection of human rights require the creation of a more responsive and accountable government and a more pluralistic and independent society. Democracy embodies the set of institutions that best guarantee political responsiveness and social pluralism. To most Americans, the sponsorship of democratic reforms seems to be a reasonable, even unassailable, position for the United States to take.

But Americans need to understand the limitations to this definition of the problem. First, successful and sustained democratization requires a variety of accompanying institutional and cultural preconditions. Higher levels of income, the emergence of a middle class independent of the state, higher levels of education, the development of a culture of mutual tolerance (what is often called a civic culture) are all preconditions for democratization, and take time to develop. In short, although democracy is not necessarily a prerequisite for economic modernization, economic development and the cultural changes that such development produces may be a condition for successful democratization. . . .

Second, Americans should not be naive about the consequences of democracy. There is a strong tendency in the United States to believe that "all good things go together"—that democratization will promote free markets, free trade, and peaceful foreign policy. Indeed, the Clinton administration's rationale for its efforts to "enlarge" the number of democracies around the world has been the assertion that democratization will promote international stability and prosperity. And yet, more recent research suggests a different possibility. Democratization, especially in immature societies, can permit the expression of nationalism that authoritarian regimes once suppressed, and thus may not lead to peaceful foreign policies. Moreover, democratic states can well adopt protectionist measures, high corporate and societal subsidies, and other policies that can contradict the principles of free trade and can restrict economic growth. And, if not conducted properly, democratic reforms can lead to social disorder and political instability. Thus democratization should be regarded as only one objective of American policy toward China, not as the only one. In particular, the U.S. should be sensitive to the traditional Chinese preoccupation with maintaining political order during periods of dynamic societal and economic change.

Third, Americans should realize that many foreigners, including Chinese, view American-style democracy as having serious flaws. They believe that pluralistic, competitive democratic institutions tend to exaggerate the differences among political forces, rather than building consensus. As a result, the policy-making process can become fragmented, contentious, and eventually gridlocked. In addition, they also believe that the high cost of lobbying and campaigning in the United States produces a kind of "money politics" that advantages the wealthy and powerful, while handicapping the ordinary citizen. To those who view democracy, like any other political system, as a means to an end, rather than an end in itself, those are powerful objections. American refusal to acknowledge these problems makes the United States appear insincere and highly ideological.

Finally, Americans will also have to acknowledge that their own model of democracy has such unusual features that it may not be frequently replicated abroad. The American system—a directly elected president combining the roles of head of state and head of government, a considerable sharing of power between the executive branch and the legislature, a strong independent judiciary, a federal relationship between the central government and the states, and single-seat districts in the legislature—is highly distinctive. As China embarks on political reform, it is highly likely that it will look elsewhere for models of political structure. . . .

International Conventions

3. Beijing should acknowledge that the international community is governed by an international regime on human rights, in much of which China already participates.

Matters of governance can no longer be considered to be protected by the principle of absolute sovereignty. There is a growing body of international law, including several international conventions, that specifies the human rights that should be universally protected. There are both global and, in some places, regional institutions that assess the performance of national governments in protecting and advancing human rights. There is also ample precedent for the international community to take action, including sanctions, against governments that engage in gross violations of human rights.

China has already accepted the legitimacy of much of this international regime. It has ratified several of the most important international conventions on human rights. It participates in the United Nations Human Rights Commission, and engages in that body in critical assessments of other nations' human rights records. And by implementing international sanctions against the former apartheid regime in South Africa, China has accepted the appropriateness of sanctions against governments that severely infringe on human rights, and the legitimate authority of intergovernmental organizations to impose such sanctions.

It would be extremely helpful to the management of the human rights issue in Sino-American relations if China were to accede to the remaining international covenants on human rights, particularly the International Covenant on Economic, Social, and Cultural Rights and the International Covenant on Civil and Political Rights. Americans should be aware that their own government ratified the second of these two international conventions only recently [1992] and has not yet ratified the first. As signatories to those conventions, both China and the United States would have to engage in regular self-examinations of their own human rights records, as well as criticize the records of other states. They would also have to subject their behavior to potential scrutiny by the United Nations Human Rights Commission. This would place the issue of human rights in a more multilateral setting, and would provide a common set of criteria for discussions of each other's human rights record.

Chinese Political Reform

4. *China should continue a gradual program of political reform, based upon the realization that genuine stability in advanced societies is rooted in responsive political institutions.*

The recent history of Sino-American relations shows that the human rights issue can be more easily managed if China is implementing a program of political reform, albeit gradual and even halting. In the mid-1980s, as noted above, China's violations of human rights began to become an issue in Beijing's relations with the United States. And yet the human rights issue was manageable at first, among other reasons because Chinese leaders before the Tiananmen crisis appeared committed to steady political reform.

It would be helpful, therefore, if Chinese leaders were to recommit themselves to a program of political reform, such as that approved by the 13th Congress of the Chinese Communist party in 1987. Such a program would be intended to build more responsive, more effective, less corrupt, and less arbitrary political institutions. These institutions would include competitive elections for government positions, a more powerful legislature, a stronger judicial system, a better trained civil service, a freer press, and nongovernmental organizations with access to decision makers. An appropriate program of political reform would also allow the emergence of a more pluralistic society, with greater autonomy from government control. As noted above, some of these reforms are already underway, but they have not been combined into a comprehensive package.

Beijing should not undertake political reform simply to appease or mollify the United States. Instead, it should do so from an understanding that political reform is a necessary concomitant of successful economic modernization, especially when economic development results from a strategy that allows private enterprise, integration with the outside world, and extensive market forces. By denying the need for such a program of political change, Chinese leaders are only exacerbating the danger that their political system will eventually be swamped by social and political contradictions. Conversely, as will be noted below, by launching such a program, Chinese leaders will be building the institutions that are the key to genuine stability and that increase the prospects for maintaining long-term public support. . . .

Common Ground

5. *China and the United States should identify areas of common ground on human rights, and work together to promote human rights in their two countries.*

On the basis of the preceding four points, China and the United States would have begun to transform the human rights issue from disagreement and confrontation to partial consensus and cooperation. They would have agreed that governments are responsible for promoting a wide range of human rights—social, economic, political, and civil. They would have agreed that those human rights are identified and protected by a body of international law. They would have agreed that governments are obliged, under that system of international law, to engage in self-criticism of their own human rights record, as well as being empowered to criticize the human rights violations of others. They would have agreed that the evaluation of any country's record must take all those human rights into account, not just a few. And they would have agreed that China needs both stability and gradual political reform.

On that basis, the two societies—including both governments and nongovernmental organizations—could engage in collaborative activities, both conceptual and practical, on the issue of human rights:

- On the conceptual level, Chinese and Americans could engage in a dialogue on the most appropriate definition of universal human rights, and on the institutional mechanisms for protecting and promoting them. The aim would be to contribute to what the Japanese scholar Onuma Yasuaki has called an " intercivilizational consensus" on human rights, in which Asian and Western societies reach a new agreement on the matter, rather than simply adopting Western values and institutions to Asian circumstances.

• Chinese and Americans could undertake more balanced and comprehensive assessment of the state of human rights in their two countries, featuring not only criticisms of each others' shortcomings, but also self-assessments of their own records. The United States should, to the greatest degree possible, avoid double standards in its evaluations of China's human rights records. That is, it should not criticize China for suppressing dissent in Tibet if it ignores the similar suppression of separatism by the Russian government in Chechnya. Nor should it fail to praise China for the economic achievements that it would recognize in other countries.

• Chinese and Americans could also develop cooperative programs to promote human rights, building on some activities already underway. This could involve promoting the rule of law, civil service reform, local elections, and legislative development in China. It could also involve joint efforts to develop poorer regions, to protect the rights of children, and to enhance the status of women and minorities. In this way, the United States will be seen as providing significant assistance to support positive developments in China, not just offering criticism of the remaining shortcomings. . . .

Managing Disagreements

6. *Both countries should also develop guidelines for managing the disagreements over human rights that will inevitably remain. . . .*

In addition to these chronic disagreements, even more contentious human rights issues may reemerge in Sino–American relations in the years ahead. Other than the emergence and suppression of political dissent in Hong Kong after the return to Chinese sovereignty in 1997, the most likely circumstance would be serious instability in China, accompanied by calls for more rapid political reform and democratization, followed by suppression of dissent in the name of stability. Given the uncertainties surrounding the succession to Deng Xiaoping [Deng died in 1997], the possibility of a downturn in the Chinese economy, and the grievances produced by inequality, inflation, corruption, and unemployment, such a scenario cannot be ruled out.

In the event of such a crisis, it is important that the two countries—and especially the United States—keep the broader picture in mind. In particular, since the crisis would likely feature the suppression of political freedoms and civil rights in China, Americans should continue to weigh the importance of economic growth, social progress, and political stability in determining the welfare of the Chinese people. Americans also need to consider whether such a crisis involves sustained retrogression from political reform, or only a temporary setback. At the same time, given that the United States will be attempting to determine the significance of a domestic political crisis in China, it is important that Chinese leaders reconfirm their commitment to gradual but sustained political reform as soon as it is feasible to do so.

China's Relations with the United States

By Wang Jisi

Wang Jisi, director of the Institute of American Studies at Beijing's Chinese Academy of Social Sciences, contends that relations between China and the United States have been strained by America's arrogant attitude and aggressive stance toward China. He argues that although the Chinese admire much about American society, various American foreign policies and actions have left them distrustful of U.S. intentions abroad. These actions include U.S. arms sales to Taiwan, the bombing of the Chinese embassy in Yugoslavia in 1999, and American criticism of China's human rights record.

In a recent survey of Chinese attitudes toward America, the respondents—a cross-section of Chinese society—were asked to give the first words that came to mind at the mention of the United States. Thirty-four percent of them answered "modernization," "affluence," or "high-tech"; 11.6 percent said "democracy" or "freedom"; and 29 percent responded "overbearing," "hegemonic," "arrogant," or "the world's policeman."

The sum of those responses is a fair representation of China's ambivalent sentiments about America, a nation whose name translates literally into Chinese as "Beautiful Country" (Meiguo). When the Chinese focus on America within its own boundaries, they see a nation that is beautifully developed, governed, and maintained. But when they view the United States as a player on the international scene, most Chinese see an unattractive and malign presence. The Chinese are similarly ambivalent about what they assume to be America's attitude toward China. Sixty percent of the respondents in the survey said they thought that America supports the process of reform and opening that is taking place in China, but an equal number said that the United States wants to prevent China from becoming a great power. They believe that Americans will accept only a China that goes the American way—and will hinder the nation's development if it does not.

Not all Chinese hold similar views of the United States. Chinese society today is increasingly pluralized, and the China-U.S. relationship is increasingly multifaceted. Yet to most Chinese—the general public and the political elites—American condescension toward China and the contrast between America's internal achievements and its external mischief are striking and puzzling.

At a closed-door meeting in Beijing, the editor of a leading Chinese newspaper expressed his feelings this way: "So far as its domestic conditions are concerned, the United States is a very good country. It is prosperous, powerful, and rich, and its living conditions are comfortable and humane. Americans have managed their country successfully. So why do we not want them to meddle in international affairs? Why are we so reluctant to learn from their experiences in running the country? Because they are too arrogant and too highhanded to be tolerated."

To be sure, the editor's comments were not entirely "politically correct." Since the founding of the People's Republic, the textbook definition of the United States has been that it is a capitalist country where the bourgeoisie exploits and oppresses the proletariat and where racial tensions reflect that class struggle. But because countless numbers of Chinese have recently made their way onto American soil as tourists, and many more have gotten ideas about America through publications, films and television, and the Internet, the official ideological line may or may not be relevant.

The Chinese debate among themselves as to whether the confusing outcome of the American presidential election in 2000 reflected a dirty power game in a pseudodemocracy or a fair competition based on the rule of law and self-government. Many Chinese youngsters are fascinated by Bill Gates, Mariah Carey, Harrison Ford, and Michael Jordan. At the same time, serious observers point to school shootings, drug addiction, police brutality, and the disparity between rich and poor as evidence of what they call the "American disease."

Global Affairs

But if the Chinese people view U.S. domestic affairs with favorable or mixed feelings, they take a quite negative view of the role and behavior of the United States in global affairs. They do not accept America's assertion that it acts in the world only on moral principles. They believe that self-interest drives U.S. foreign policy no less than it drives the foreign policy of any other nation. They point out that even American leaders justify U.S. international actions by invoking the national interest, as when President Richard Nixon said during his historic visit in 1972 that he had come to China in the interests of the United States. In 1991, President George Bush launched the Persian Gulf War to safeguard the Middle East oil supply, and not, as he asserted, to create a "new world order." In Rwanda and other strife-torn countries, Washington has taken few steps to help because it sees little to gain.

It is especially difficult for the Chinese to accept the notion Americans have of their "manifest destiny"—that they are the people chosen by God to save the rest of the world for democracy and freedom. In China's largely atheist society, the American propensity to interfere on the international stage seems no more than a camouflaged ambition to acquire fortune and power. The 1999 military action in Kosovo by the North Atlantic Treaty Organization (NATO), for example, was widely perceived in China as an American scheme—under the guise of protecting human rights—to conquer Yugoslavia, isolate Russia, weaken the European Union, warn China, and, ultimately, keep the United States in a dominant position.

American Attitudes

Some Chinese with a liberal, cosmopolitan outlook, who may not be so critical of America's motivation or its alleged greediness for power, are nonetheless disturbed by America's attitude. The Confucian tradition regards modesty as a virtue and presumption as a sin. The United States, in their eyes, is guilty of assuming too much. They particularly resent members of the U.S. Congress who know little about international issues yet attempt to impose sanctions on other nations.

The vast majority of Chinese observers reject the U.S. notion that America should "play a leadership role" in the world—both because they see that role as self-assumed and because the word leadership in the Chinese language connotes a hierarchical order in which many are subordinated to one. In their view, the United States should "mind its own business"—and remedy the various manifestations of social and moral decay at home before it denounces others.

Books and Hollywood movies are windows on America for the Chinese, and, for better or worse, they effectively shape America's image in China. A lot of American movies reveal the dirty side of U.S. politics and society, even as they extol the virtuous side. But when the plots involve the international scene or imaginary star wars, Americans as a group are heroes and saviors, while the peoples of other nations are either followers of Americans (in which case, they must be "good guys") or anti-American devils (who have to be eliminated). The U.S. news media tend to make judgments along the same lines: the lives and well-being of U.S. citizens are by definition more valuable than those of foreigners—friends and foes alike. Americans have a system of values; others have ideologies. Loyalty to America is "patriotism," loyalty in other countries is merely "nationalism."

Chinese commentators on international security issues observe that the United States possesses by far the most formidable armed forces in the world. Yet at a time when the world is basically at peace, America is increasing its military budget. The commentators refuse to buy the argument that a missile defense system, if developed by Americans, would not be threatening to other nations. The ostensibly defensive system, they believe, would embolden policymakers in Washington to take the offensive against potential rivals and deprive them of their defense capabilities. In other words, Americans want the luxury of "absolute security," and they are prepared to achieve it by making other nations even more vulnerable.

In Chinese eyes, the world would be a safer and fairer place if the United States, China, Russia, the European states, Japan, and many other countries shared responsibility for dealing with global and regional issues through multilateral consultations in settings such as the United Nations. Unfortunately, the world today is becoming increasingly unbalanced because international norms and institutions seem so much to favor the United States.

Economic Affairs
Economic globalization has clearly benefited China. Millions of Chinese welcome the presence of Coke, McDonald's, Motorola,

Microsoft, Disney, Reebok, and companies like them, and they earn good salaries working on the production lines of Western companies. But millions of other Chinese, particularly those working in state-owned enterprises that face fierce competition from American industrial giants, may lose their jobs. Because Americans are in China to make money, and not out of a sense of charity, few Chinese feel grateful to the United States for the improvement in U.S.-China economic relations.

American Attempts to Weaken China

For the Chinese, the United States is, at once, their greatest economic partner and their gravest external threat. It does not much matter to them how the United States is governed, or even how it conducts its global affairs generally. What does matter is America's attitude specifically toward the growth of China's national power.

The official Chinese line is that U.S. strategy is designed to Westernize, divide, and weaken China. Despite the obvious political motivation for such an allegation, the belief is widespread in China that the United States does indeed want to keep the country down for strategic purposes—and is not hostile merely to the communist leadership in Beijing. As one Chinese student of international relations has remarked, "I am puzzled by what the Americans have done to China. They say they do not like the Chinese government but are friendly to the Chinese people. That is understandable from a political perspective. But they have obstructed the Chinese bid for holding the Olympics in Beijing, threatened to revoke normal trade relations between the two countries, and shown little concern about the suffering in China from devastating floods. They try to dissuade China from selling weapons to the countries they dislike, even as they sell advanced weapons to Taiwan to strengthen its position against China's reunification. So do they really want to hurt the Chinese government only, or do they want to harm the Chinese nation as a whole?"

The Taiwan issue feeds the Chinese suspicion that the United States is pursuing a strategy of "divide and rule." It evokes the collective memory of China's being bullied and dismembered by Japan and the Western powers for more than a century after the Opium War. In 1950, at the outbreak of the Korean War, the Truman administration dispatched the U.S. Seventh Fleet to the Taiwan Strait. In the Chinese interpretation, that act and the subsequent U.S. support of Taiwan have kept the island separated from the mainland for more than 50 years.

Perpetuating the separation may serve several U.S. interests. First, by keeping China's territory divided and its sovereignty violated, the United States may hamper China's drive to achieve the dignity of a great power. Second, Taiwan's ongoing acquisition of U.S. weaponry is good business for U.S. military industries. Third, continued tensions across the Taiwan Strait provide an excuse for Americans to maintain a military presence in the Asian Pacific and to develop their missile projects. Finally, by endorsing Taiwan's democratization, Washington may exert more pressure on Beijing for political change. All these Chinese fears and interpretations of events persist in the face of assurances from the United States that its commitment to the security of Taiwan is morally motivated and intended to do nothing more than maintain peace in the area.

NATO Bombing and Human Rights

In the wake of the NATO bombing of China's embassy in Belgrade on May 8, 1999, Chinese policy analysts and scholars heatedly debated the status of China-U.S. relations and how China should respond to America's neo-interventionism. Although pragmatic considerations in favor of stabilizing relations with Washington have thus far prevailed in Beijing, the bombing had a devastating effect. Government officials joined the general public in expressing their indignation—along with their perplexity as to why the bombing had occurred. In the survey cited at the start of this essay, 85 percent of the respondents said they were convinced that the bombing had been deliberate.

Many Chinese are likewise disturbed by the condescending and overbearing tone of American criticism of China's human rights record. They are ready to concede, at least privately, that the human rights situation in China is far from satisfactory. But they suspect that the criticisms are politically motivated. Some Chinese point out that Americans were virtually silent when the human rights situation in China was at its worst, during the Cultural Revolution (1966–76), whereas they vigorously reproach China today, when the situation has improved remarkably. One explanation for the odd behavior is that the United States needed China in the past to counter the Soviet Union—and needs a new enemy today to continue the Cold War.

Chinese Ambivalence

In any case, China's ambivalence about the "Beautiful Country" will linger. Deep in the Chinese mind lurks a strange combination of images of America—a repressive hegemon, a sentimental imperialist, a grave threat, a hypocritical crusader, a contagious disease, a successful polity, a gorgeous land, a ravishing culture, an indispensable partner, a fond dream, and a patronizing teacher.

Chinese political elites may still recall the striking remarks made by Mao Zedong in 1949, when he referred to the West as a dream and as a teacher: "Imperialist aggression shattered the fond dreams of the Chinese about learning from the West. It was very odd—why were the teachers always committing aggression against the pupil? The Chinese learned a great deal from the West, but they could never make it work and were never able to realize their ideals." Hence, the revolution to drive the West out of China.

The process of reform and opening that is now occurring in China can be seen as the renewal of an earlier painful process of learning from the West. Many Chinese wonder whether the teachers will once again bully the pupil. And yet, how immeasurably better it will be—for the United States and for the rest of the world—if, in the 21st century, Chinese ideals are fulfilled.

The Struggle for the Fate of Taiwan

By David Curtis Wright

A unified China has been the goal of every Chinese government from the first emperor Qin Shihuang up to the present one under Jiang Zemin. Taiwan is part of that plan. Taiwan was under Japanese control for many years. When Japan was defeated in World War II, Taiwan returned to Chinese control. At the end of the Chinese civil war in 1949, General Chiang Kai-shek and his Nationalist troops fled mainland China and moved the government of the Republic of China to Taiwan, where Chiang ruled as a dictator. Chiang maintained until his death in 1975 that his was the legitimate government of China.

By the 1970s, most Western democracies had recognized the People's Republic of China (PRC) in Beijing as the legitimate government of China. The United States broke off relations with Taiwan in 1979 and recognized the PRC. After Chiang Kai-shek's death, Taiwan began to evolve toward democracy, although it did not hold an openly democratic election for president until 1996.

The Chinese government under Jiang Zemin's leadership seeks to return Taiwan to the motherland. Beijing has threatened a military invasion if Taiwan formally declares independence, if a foreign country invades, or if reunification is postponed indefinitely. A Chinese military invasion could bring the United States into the conflict. The United States supports Taiwan's democratization process, but it also wants to maintain good relations with Beijing. Many analysts consider Taiwan as the issue most likely to cause a war between China and the United States. David Curtis Wright, assistant professor of history at the University of Calgary, Alberta, Canada, reviews the past fifty years of Taiwan's history and the current unification controversy. This selection is from his book The History of China.

David Curtis Wright, *The History of China*. New York: W.W. Norton & Company, 2001. Copyright © 2001 by David Curtis Wright. Reproduced by permission.

C hina lacks the will, ideology, and historical experience necessary to dominate the globe militarily and economically the way the United States has since the end of World War II. Nevertheless, between China and the United States there does exist a potentially volatile flashpoint, one based much more on reality than the half-baked conspiracy musings of ultra-conservative crackpots: the ultimate fate of the island of Taiwan. Taiwan has been separated from mainland China by civil war since 1949, but the government of the mainland is bound and determined to bring Taiwan back into its fold, peacefully if possible but by force if necessary. Taiwan, for its part, is much less enthusiastic about reunification with the mainland and seems to want to postpone it indefinitely. At the dawn of the twenty-first century, the ultimate fate of Taiwan remains one of the world's great unresolved geopolitical issues. . . .

Iron-Fist Rule

Safely beyond the reach of the Chinese Communists on the mainland and hiding behind the skirts of the U.S. military, Chiang Kai-shek insisted until his death in 1975 that his military and government would one day return to the mainland in triumph and cleanse it of Communist occupation. He stubbornly regarded his as the sole legitimate government of all of China and the Communists on the mainland as mere "Communist bandits" *(gongfei)* who would one day be exterminated. Generations of soldiers in Taiwan were inducted into the Nationalist armed forces and indoctrinated with this unrealistic hope. Until around 1987, political and military slogans about one day returning to the mainland and defeating the Communists were plastered everywhere: on government buildings, street signs, school walls, and even mailboxes. Chiang Kai-shek suspended participatory democracy in Taiwan indefinitely because of the "national emergency" involving "Communist bandit insurgency" on the mainland. The ragtag remnants of his central government and various provincial governments ran the entire show, and the tiny number of officials from Taiwan he allowed to be elected into his government and rubber-stamp legislature made little significant difference in the formulation of government policy. Chiang ruled Taiwan with an iron fist and promptly clapped anyone who criticized him or his government in jail. His government controlled all newspapers, television stations, and radio broadcasts and encouraged people to inform anonymously on "Communist troublemakers" (*feidie*, literally "bandit agents")....

Incredibly, many countries supported Chiang's fiction of being the only legitimate government of all China, of which Taiwan was a part, until well into the 1960s and 1970s. Britain, never a fan of Chiang Kai-shek's government, had recognized the People's Republic immediately after its founding [in 1949], but most other major countries continued to recognize the Nationalists. In 1965 France cut off relations with Chiang's government and extended diplomatic recognition to mainland China. Canada and Japan followed suit in the early 1970s, and in 1972 the Nationalists were expelled from the United Nations and replaced by representatives from the People's Republic. Chiang Kai-shek flew into a rage over this and angrily predicted that the United Nations would soon collapse because of its perfidious expulsion of his government. By the mid-1970s most of the industrialized democracies of the world had, with the exception of the United States, faced up to reality, broken off relations with Taiwan, and recognized the People's Republic of China and *its* claim to be the only legal government of China, of which Taiwan was a part. In the early 1970s the Americans made tentative overtures to the Chinese Communists, and anyone who could sense the directions of the political winds of the time could tell that the United States would eventually recognize the PRC. Chiang Kai-shek did not live to see the final break with the Americans. He died a deeply frustrated and disappointed man in 1975, probably knowing that his government would finally forsake his dream of recovering the mainland. On December 15, 1978, President Jimmy Carter finally announced the United States' break with Taiwan and pending normalization of relations with mainland China, which would be effective on January 1, 1979....

Chiang Ching-kuo, son of Chiang Kai-shek and president of the Republic of China on Taiwan from 1978 to 1988, must be given a portion of the credit for fostering the transition to genuine democracy in Taiwan. He took a significant step toward the reconciliation of the island's mainlander and native populations by appointing Lee Teng-hui (Li Denghui in the spelling system preferred in mainland China), a native Taiwanese with a Ph.D. in agricultural economics from Cornell, as his vice president. He also eased up on many of his father's more draconian policies and perceptibly toned down the back-to-the-mainland rhetoric, although he continued to excoriate the Chinese Communists during his entire tenure as president. . . .

Democracy Emerges

When Chiang Ching-kuo died in 1988, Taiwan began its raucous transition to full democracy. Lee Teng-hui eventually succeeded Chiang Ching-kuo as president of the Republic of China, and a relatively new political party, the Democratic Progressive Party (DPP), began more aggressively asserting itself and challenging (sometimes directly and even physically) the island's Kuomintang government to democratize itself. The Kuomintang, which by this time was dominated by native-born Taiwanese, eventually gave in and began democratizing itself. The transition from essentially one-party rule to authentic democracy was brief but intense and highly confrontational. Fistfights and even gang fights frequently broke out on the floor of Taiwan's legislature, right under a gigantic portrait of Sun Yat-sen, as members of the DPP, Kuomintang, and other parties struggled to learn how to disagree with one another in a peaceful and civilized manner. . . .

In 1996 Taiwan held its first openly democratic and popular election for the president of the Republic of China. Prior to this time, the president was appointed by the government; even Lee Teng-hui's elevation to the presidency upon the death of Chiang Ching-kuo was the result of succession, not election. Lee Teng-hui had vowed to hold an open and democratic election for the presidency, and in 1996 this became a reality. The Communist leaders of mainland China, always fearful of direct democratic elections, watched nervously as the people of Taiwan excitedly participated for the first time in all of Chinese history in a genuinely democratic and popular election of a Chinese national leader. The free speech of the campaign unnerved the Communist rulers and led them to fear that widespread sentiment in favor of Taiwan's formal independence might be given popular and legitimate expression in the election. Mainland Chinese news broadcasters, failing utterly to understand the momentous significance of the democratic nature of the election, warned Taiwan not to harbor ambitions of formally breaking away from China because of its "excuse" of having "changed its style of selecting its president." Lee, for his part, publicly stated during the campaign that the mainland was "crazy in the head" (a phrase he spoke in Japanese) over the election and his visit to Cornell the year before.

Highly distressed by all of this and suspicious that Lee was secretly scheming for independence, the mainland launched a crude campaign of intimidation aimed squarely at Taiwan's voting public. Mainland Chinese warships plied the waters near Taiwan and "test fired" several missiles in the general direction of the island. Their purpose was to create panic and fear in Taiwan and goad the island's population into backing away from their pending election of Lee Teng-hui. This clumsy demonstration of brute force showed just how little the mainland rulers really knew and understood Taiwan's people, and their actions produced the opposite effect. Support for Lee actually *increased* during this time, especially after he traveled to the Pescadores (a groups of islands midway between Taiwan and the mainland) and defiantly shook his fist at the mainland, proclaiming that nobody was frightened of its scare tactics. U.S. President Bill Clinton jumped into the fray by sending two carrier battle groups from the U.S. Seventh Fleet (stationed in Japan) into the waters off Taiwan in a show of force against the mainland vessels attempting to intimidate the island. This action enraged the Chinese leadership, and soon the inevitable accusations of U.S. connivance in Taiwan's elections were flying. In the end, however, the Chinese warships backed off and returned to port, and the situation blew over. Hotheads in the mainland nursed a growing grudge against the United States for its influence in the region, while in Taiwan some advocates of Taiwanese independence began to believe, perhaps unrealistically, that the action proved that the United States would never stand idly by and allow the mainland Chinese military to invade or seriously menace their island.

Continuing Tensions

Tensions between the mainland and Taiwan were once again heightened in mid-1999, when President Lee announced in an interview broadcast over German radio that he and his government would now conduct talks and contacts with the Communist government on the mainland only on the basis of government-to-government relations. In doing so Lee was simply emphasizing the obvious facts that two governments on either side of the Taiwan Strait did in fact exist and that the Republic of China had been a reality since 1912. To the mainland, this was an ominous step closer to a formal declaration of independence. Given the mainland's recent belligerent mood and saber rattling, Lee's "one country, two governments" formulation was precipitous and ill-advised. It has only increased suspicion and heightened tensions in the Taiwan Strait, across which fundamental misunderstanding exists in both directions.

Tensions flared up once again in February 2000, when the mainland Chinese government issued a white paper making new threats to Taiwan. Like mainland China's saber rattling in early 1996, these new threats occurred on the eve of democratic presidential elections on Taiwan and were clearly intended to intimidate and bully the island's voting population into selecting a candidate pleasing to Beijing. The Chinese Communists were clearly unnerved by the possibility of a pro-independence candidate winning the election and taking Taiwan even farther down the road of formal independence. The three candidates running were Lien Chan (President Lee's vice president; Lian Zhan in the spelling system preferred on the mainland); Chen Shui-bian (Chen Shuibian), a native Taiwanese and member of the DPP who had declared that Taiwan already *was* a sovereign state and did not need to declare it formally; and James Soong (Song Chuyu), a former member of the Kuomintang who now ran as an independent and generally favored closer ties with the mainland. Of these three candidates, James Soong was obviously the most suitable as far as Beijing was concerned, and Lien Chan, even though he had been Lee Teng-hui's vice president, was certainly more acceptable than the pro-independence choice Chen Shui-bian. Chen Shui-bian won the election with 39 percent of the popular vote. James Soong finished right behind him with 37 percent; and Lien Chan came in a distant third at 23 percent. The remaining 1 percent of the vote went to minor also-rans. . . .

The previous blustering from the mainland had consistently emphasized that Taiwan would be invaded if one of two situations developed: a formal declaration of independence, or foreign invasion of the island. In February 2000 a third condition was added: indefinite postponement of unification. Taiwan loomed very large in Jiang Zemin's thinking about his historical legacy. Mao and Deng both made great contributions to China: Mao had liberated China from Chiang Kai-shek and foreign imperialists, and Deng had stopped Mao's ruinous mass movements and brought relative prosperity by opening China to trade and contact with the outside world. Jiang was the third major leader of the People's Republic of China; what would his historical contributions be? Jiang noted with satisfaction that the return of Hong Kong in mid-1997 and Macao in late 1999 had both occurred during his rule. The reunification of China would be his legacy, along with the continuation of Deng Xiaoping's policies. Only Taiwan remained beyond Beijing's grasp, and Jiang was determined that he would also bring the island back to the motherland during his rule. Taiwan's continued resistance to Beijing's overtures was a source of frustration and vexation for Jiang Zemin and China's other Communist leaders as the year 2000 dawned in China and around the world.

Different Views of Unification

Mainland China grossly overestimates Taiwan's desires for unification with the motherland. In Taiwan today a large majority of the population would favor independence for their island if it could be achieved without provoking an armed attack from the mainland. It is an open secret that Lee Teng-hui favors independence but cannot possibly say so publicly. Taiwan today has good reason for not being enthusiastic about unification with the mainland in the near future. Taiwan in the 1990s was light-years ahead of the mainland in terms of prosperity, democracy, respect for human rights, and freedom of expression. The island does struggle with some measure of corruption and organized crime, but the overwhelming majority of its people would be quite unwilling to trade their newfound democracy, freedom, and prosperity for any form of mainland-style authoritarian government that might take harsh moves to improve social stability. Taiwan will not react passively if faced with invasion from the mainland; its people will stoutly resist any Communist invasion and may well surprise the world with their military might and capability. Such a scenario would post an enormous quandary to the United States, which heartily approves of Taiwan's recent democratization and prosperity and yet greatly desires harmonious diplomatic relations with China, the world's most populous state and potentially America's largest market. The U.S. Seventh Fleet is stationed in Japan, and the question for the Americans would be whether to intervene.

Taiwan, for its part, grossly underestimates the mainland's total determination and commitment to bring Taiwan back into its grasp, by force if necessary. The mainland rulers are well aware of, and distressed by, public opinion in Taiwan that favors independence for the island. But public opinion on Taiwan will not alter their plans to absorb the island because they have an even more awesome consideration in mind: the momentum of history. Since its first unification under the Qin in 221 B.C. China has placed an enormous premium on national unity. At the end of the twentieth century, Hong Kong and Macao have returned to Chinese sovereignty, and Taiwan is the last piece of historically Chinese territory left for the People's Republic to recover. As much as the government of the People's Republic of China would like to, it cannot proclaim at the dawn of the twenty-first century that its great enterprise of achieving complete national unity is accomplished. Much to its frustration, the mainland government cannot even point to a timetable for an orderly transition to national unification; that remains an elusive goal. Taiwan's continual quasi-independence from the People's Republic is a painful thorn in the side for all mainland Chinese patriots. The mainland will not let Taiwan go without a tooth-and-nail fight, and it seems that if the people of Taiwan truly desire independence from the mainland, they must admit that they are in fact cutting off their historical ties with mainland China and then prepare themselves for a very long and disruptive battle with mainland invaders. They must neither underestimate the determination and military ability of the People's Republic to resist their moves toward independence nor naively expect Uncle Sam to rush to their rescue in their hour of need. The United States might elect to stay out of the fight and wait to see what comes of it. American intervention in a battle across the Taiwan Strait could very well lead to a larger war between China and the United States, which would mean tremendous losses for both sides, especially for China. China's economic development would be ruined and set back twenty years or more, and mass starvation would likely break out in China after the disruption of its transportation and communication infrastructure. The United States would probably prevail in any armed conflict with China not involving a ground war, but the cost in blood and treasure for such a victory might ultimately prove higher than the American public is willing to tolerate.

Chronology

ca. 2205–1766 B.C.
The Xia dynasty rules China.

ca. 1766–1122 B.C.
The Shang dynasty rules China; the first Chinese writing appears.

1122–256 B.C.
The Zhou dynasty rules China as a feudal state.

221–206 B.C.
The Qin dynasty rules China, and the nation is unified for the first time.

202 B.C.–A.D. 220
The Han dynasty rules China and adopts Confucianism as its official ideology.

220–589
The Period of Division follows the fall of the Han dynasty; national unity disintegrates.

589–618
The Sui dynasty reunites China under one rule.

618–907
The Tang dynasty rules as a wealthy and powerful empire; Chang'an, the Tang capital, is the largest city in the world.

907–960
Five dynasties and ten kingdoms follow the decline of the Tang dynasty.

960–1279
The Song dynasty rules China.

1279–1368
The Yuan dynasty is established when the Mongols invade and conquer China.

1368–1644
The Ming dynasty reestablishes Han Chinese rule.

1644–1912
The Qing dynasty is established by Manchurians.

1717
Lhasa (Tibet) is incorporated into the Qing empire.

1796–1804
The White Lotus Rebellion begins as a religious movement and becomes a political uprising against the Qing dynasty.

1839–1842
The First Opium War occurs: China attempts to stop Great Britain's illegal importation of opium, and Britain counters with military action. China is defeated in the ensuing war.

1842
The Treaty of Nanjing ends the First Opium War; China is forced to open ports and cede Hong Kong to the British.

1850–1864
The Taiping Rebellion led by Hong Xiuquan leads to civil war; although the uprising is repressed, the Qing dynasty is weakened and made vulnerable to foreign imperialism.

1856–1858
The Second Opium War ends with the Treaty of Tientsin (1858) in which China makes additional concessions to European imperial intruders.

1894–1895
During the Sino-Japanese War, China loses domination of Korea to Japan.

1898
During the Hundred Days Reform, the Qing emperor tries to transform China into a constitutional monarchy but is thwarted by conservatives led by the Empress Dowager Cixi.

1900

The Boxer Rebellion, a popular movement that uses violence to drive foreigners from China, occurs.

1908

The Empress Dowager Cixi and the Guangxu emperor die; the last Qing emperor, Pu Yi, ascends the throne.

1911

A revolution against the Qing dynasty breaks out; Sun Yat-sen is recognized as the leader of the revolutionary movement.

1912

The Qing emperor abdicates, and the Republic of China is established.

1912–1916

Yuan Shikai is president of the Republic of China; he attempts to establish himself as a new emperor but dies before he can accomplish the task.

1916–1927

After Yuan Shikai dies, China is ruled by regional warlords (known as the Warlord Era).

1919

Beijing university students demonstrate against Japanese imperialism in a patriotic show of Chinese nationalism known as the May Fourth Movement.

1920

Sun Yat-sen establishes the Nationalist Party (Guomindang).

1921

The Chinese Communist Party is founded.

1924

The Nationalist Party holds its first congress.

1925

Sun Yat-sen dies and Chiang Kai-shek emerges as the new Nationalist Party leader.

1926–1928

Chiang Kai-shek leads troops against regional warlords in the Northern Expedition.

1931

Japan occupies Manchuria after invading Chinese territory.

1932

The Japanese puppet state of Manchukuo is established, and the last Qing emperor, Pu Yi, is installed as head of state.

1934–1935

Chiang Kai-shek attempts to eliminate Communist rivals; the Communists retreat in the arduous and legendary Long March from their south base to northern China.

1935

Mao Zedong takes over leadership of the Chinese Communist Party during the Long March.

1936

Regional military leaders place Chiang Kai-shek under house arrest in Xi'an until he agrees to end his struggle against the Communists and unite with them to fight Japanese invaders.

1937

Japanese troops occupy Nanjing and commit atrocities against the citizens.

1937–1945

China and Japan are at war.

1945

Japan surrenders and World War II ends.

1947–1949

Civil war breaks out between the Communists and the Nationalists. The Communists are victorious, and the Nationalists, led by Chiang Kai-shek, flee to Taiwan.

1949

The Communist Party establishes the People's Republic of China (PRC).

1950

China signs a friendship treaty with the Soviet Union; the Marriage Law, which reforms family and social relations, is announced; China enters the Korean War.

1951

Chinese troops are sent to Tibet to reunify Tibet with Han China; all resistance is suppressed.

1957

Mao initiates the One Hundred Flowers Campaign and invites criticism of Communist Party policies; he also initiates the Great Leap Forward, an economic program designed to increase agricultural and industrial productivity.

1959

Tibetans revolt against the People's Liberation Army; the uprising is suppressed, and the Dalai Lama flees to India.

1959–1961

The Great Leap Forward fails miserably; a great famine follows, and millions die of starvation.

1960

China and the Soviet Union split and end friendly relations.

1962

Border warfare breaks out between China and the Soviet Union.

1966–1976

Mao attempts to return China to revolutionary principles by encouraging the Cultural Revolution; chaos and terror reign.

1971

China is admitted into the United Nations; U.S. president Richard Nixon visits China.

1975

Chiang Kai-shek dies in Taiwan.

1976

Mao Zedong and Zhou Enlai, premier of the People's Republic of China, die within months of each other.

1978

Deng Xiaoping initiates an economic reform program and opens China to the world.

1978–1979

Chinese dissidents post statements critical of government policies on the Democracy Wall in Beijing.

1979

U.S.-Chinese diplomatic relations are normalized.

1987

An armed rebellion in Tibet is suppressed by the People's Liberation Army.

1989

Students demonstrate in favor of political reform in Beijing's Tiananmen Square; the People's Liberation Army moves in and many people are killed.

1992

The National People's Congress approves the construction of the Three Gorges Dam despite opposition by environmentalists.

1993

Jiang Zemin becomes president of the People's Republic of China.

1997

Deng Xiaoping dies; Hong Kong returns to Chinese control after more than 150 years as a British colony.

1999

Macao returns to China after more than 150 years of Portuguese control.

2002

The People's Republic of China joins the World Trade Organization.

For Further Research

General Histories of China

John K. Fairbank, *China: A New History*. Cambridge, MA: Belknap Press of Harvard University Press, 1992.

Jacques Gernet, *A History of Chinese Civilization*. Cambridge, England: Cambridge University Press, 1972.

Ray Huang, *China: A Macro History*. Armonk, NY: M.E. Sharpe, 1997.

Peter Mitchell, *China: Tradition and Revolution*. Toronto: Macmillan of Canada, 1977.

J.A.G. Roberts, *A Concise History of China*. Cambridge, MA: Harvard University Press, 1999.

David Curtis Wright, *The History of China*. Westport, CT: Greenwood Press, 2001.

Ancient, Medieval, and Early Modern China

Kwang-chih Chang, *Shang Civilization*. New Haven, CT: Yale University Press, 1980.

Arthur Cotterell, *The First Emperor of China*. New York: Holt, Rinehart, and Winston, 1981.

Denise Dersin, ed., *What Life Was Like in the Land of the Dragon: Imperial China A.D. 960–1368*. Alexandria, VA: Time-Life Books, 1998.

A.E. Dien, ed., *State and Society in Early Medieval China*. Palo Alto, CA: Stanford University Press, 1991.

P.B. Ebrey, *The Inner Quarters: Marriage and the Lives of Chinese Women in the Sung Period*. Berkeley: University of California Press, 1993.

John D. Langlois, *China Under Mongol Rule*. Princeton, NJ: Princeton University Press, 1981.

Michael Loewe, *Everyday Life in Early Imperial China During the Han Period, 202 B.C.–220 A.D.* London: Carousel Books, 1973.

Luo Zhewen and Zhao Luo, *The Great Wall of China in History and Legend*. Beijing: Foreign Languages Press, 1986.

Mark McNeilly, *Sun Tzu and the Art of Modern Warfare*. New York: Oxford University Press, 2001.

Morris Rossabi, *Khubilai Khan: His Life and Times*. Berkeley: University of California Press, 1988.

Sima Qian, *Records of the Grand Historian of China*. Trans. B. Watson. New York: Columbia University Press, 1961.

A.F. Wright, *The Sui Dynasty*. New York: Knopf, 1978.

Modern and Contemporary China

Gregor Benton and Alan Hunter, eds., *Wild Lily, Prairie Fire: China's Road to Democracy, Yan'an to Tian'anmen, 1942–1989*. Princeton, NJ: Princeton University Press, 1995.

David Bonavia, *China's Warlords*. Hong Kong and New York: Oxford University Press, 1995.

Iris Chang, *The Rape of Nanking: The Forgotten Holocaust of World War II*. New York: BasicBooks, 1997.

Da Chen, *Colors of the Mountain*. New York: Anchor Books, 2001.

Rafe De Krespigny, *China This Century*. Hong Kong and New York: Oxford University Press, 1992.

Lee Feigon, *Demystifying Tibet: Unlocking the Secrets of the Land of Snows*. Chicago: Ivan R. Dee, 1996.

Feng Jicai, *Ten Years of Madness: Oral Histories of China's Cultural Revolution*. San Francisco: China Books and Periodicals, 1996.

Joseph Fewsmith, *China Since Tiananmen: The Politics of Transition*. Cambridge, England: Cambridge University Press, 2001.

Ji Li Jiang, *Red Scarf Girl: A Memoir of the Cultural Revolution.* New York: HarperCollins, 1997.

Jung Chang, *Wild Swans: Three Daughters of China.* New York: Anchor Books, 1992.

Stanley Karnow, *Mao and China.* New York: Penguin, 1990.

Edwin Leung Pak-wah, ed., *Historical Dictionary of Revolutionary China.* Westport, CT: Greenwood Press, 1992.

Aisin-Gioro Pu Yi, *From Emperor to Citizen: The Autobiography of Aisin-Gioro Pu Yi.* New York: Oxford University Press, 1987.

Harrison E. Salisbury, *Tiananmen Diary: Thirteen Days in June.* Boston: Little, Brown, 1989.

Orville Schell, *Mandate of Heaven: A New Generation of Entrepreneurs, Dissidents, Bohemians, and Technocrats Lays Claim to China's Future.* New York: Simon and Schuster, 1994.

———, *Virtual Tibet: Searching for Shangri-La from the Himalayas to Hollywood.* New York: Henry Holt, 2000.

Orville Schell and David Shambaugh, *The China Reader: The Reform Era.* New York: Vintage Books, 1999.

R. Keith Schoppa, *The Columbia Guide to Modern Chinese History.* New York: Columbia University Press, 2000.

Edgar Snow, *Red Star over China.* New York: Grove Press, 1938.

Debra E. Soled, ed., *China: A Nation in Transition.* Washington, DC: Congressional Quarterly, 1995.

Jonathan D. Spence, *The Gate of Heavenly Peace: The Chinese and Their Revolution, 1895–1980.* New York: Penguin, 1981.

———, *The Search for Modern China.* New York: W.W. Norton, 1990.

Teng Ssu-Yu and John K. Fairbank, eds., *China's Response to the West: A Documentary Survey, 1839–1923.* New York: Atheneum, 1963.

Ezra F. Vogel, ed., *Living with China: U.S.-China Relations in the Twenty-First Century.* New York: W.W. Norton, 1997.

Ranbir Vohra, *China's Path to Modernization: A Historical Review from 1800 to the Present.* Upper Saddle River, NJ: Prentice-Hall, 2000.

Jan Wong, *Red China Blues: My Long March from Mao to Now.* Toronto: Doubleday/Anchor Books, 1996.

Jianying Zha, *China Pop: How Soap Operas, Tabloids, and Bestsellers Are Transforming a Culture.* New York: New Press, 1995.

Films

Beijing Bicycle and *So Close to Paradise.* Dir. Wang Xiaoshuai. Both films tell the story of two young men from the country who migrate to the city in search of a better life and the challenges they encounter.

Chungking Express. Dir. Wong Kar Wai. A whimsical look at two love affairs in Hong Kong in the years before reunification with mainland China.

Crouching Tiger, Hidden Dragon. Dir. Ang Lee. This classic *wuxia* film (martial knight/swordsman) explores the tension between the needs of the individual and the needs of the group. The title of the film is a Chinese idiom indicating a place where there are many outstanding and talented people who are "hidden," and one would be wise to seek them out. Takes place during the Qing dynasty.

The Emperor and the Assassin. Dir. Chen Kaige. Historical epic about the assassination attempt made on China's first emperor, Qin Shihuang, as documented by Han-era historian Sima Qian.

Farewell My Concubine. Dir. Chen Kaige. Two Peking Opera stars experience the major events of twentieth-century Chinese history.

Hero. Dir. Zhang Yimou. (Release set for 2003.) Explores the idea of heroism in Chinese culture. Portrays yet another assassination attempt made on China's first emperor, Qin Shihuang.

King of Masks. Dir. Wu Tianming. A traditional street performer in Sichuan in the 1930s wishes to pass on his art as "king of masks." He buys a child in a street market and is confronted with a big surprise.

The Last Emperor. Dir. B. Bertolucci. Epic film about the last Qing emperor, Henry Pu Yi, from his childhood in the Forbidden City where he was known as the Lord of 10,000 Years to his final years as a gardener in Beijing.

A Mongolian Tale. Dir. Xie Fei. Focuses on two Mongolian lovers who are separated and spend years trying to find each other again. Superb soundtrack of native Mongolian music.

Not One Less. Dir. Zhang Yimou. A very young teacher fights to keep all of her students in school so that she can get a bonus. The film shows the disparity between China's impoverished rural peasants and affluent city dwellers.

Once Upon a Time in China. (Parts 1, 2, and 3.) Dir. Tsui Hark. These three films set in Hong Kong during the final years of the Qing dynasty are about the life of Wong Fei Hung, a physician, scholar, teacher, and kung fu master who is revered for his compassion and heroism.

Project A II. Dir. Jackie Chan. A brave Hong Kong cop battles police corruption and considers joining a band of revolutionaries who are attempting to bring down the Qing emperor.

Shadow Magic. Dir. Ann Hu. Based on a true story about the introduction of moving pictures into China in 1902, with an underlying theme of the tension between duty to one's family and duty to one's art.

Shower. Dir. Zhang Yang. A young businessman who is seeking his fortune in the city returns home to visit his father and disabled brother and comes to have a new appreciation for traditional family values.

To Live. Dir. Zhang Yimou. At times tragic, at times amusing, this always compelling film follows a single family through the major events of twentieth-century Chinese history.

Xiu Xiu. Dir. Joan Chen. A young girl is "sent down" during the Cultural Revolution to the countryside. Her attempts to get the proper documents to return home lead to tragedy.

INDEX